a memoir

Bruce Ario

CITY
BOY

ISBN 13: 978-1-59298-858-7

Library of Congress Catalog Number: 2015946223

Printed in the United States of America

First Printing: 2015

19 18 17 16 15   5 4 3 2 1

Cover and interior design by Laura Drew.
Cover illustration by John Donahue.

Beaver's Pond Press
7108 Ohms Lane
Edina, MN 55439–2129
952-829-8818
www.beaverspondpress.com

I dedicate this book to my angel, Grannie.

TO LAURA,
I HOPE YOU
ENJOY READING IT
HALF AS MUCH
AS I DID
WRITING IT.
TTYL,
BRUCE

SEE THE WORLD AS YOURSELF.
HAVE FAITH IN THE WAY THINGS ARE.
LOVE THE WORLD AS YOURSELF.

—Lao Tzu, *Tao Te Ching*,
translated by Stephen Mitchell

1

IF I HAD been born in the country, it would have been different, but I was born in the city—a city boy. John Argent Jr. punctured his way out of his mother's womb, opened his eyes, and began to cry. Mrs. Argent lay in exhaustion.

"He looks like a healthy baby. You told me this is your second boy, Mrs. Argent. The second one is always the sensitive one. Perhaps he'll be an artist or a writer." The obstetrician smiled, his white coat almost pale next to the purity of the baby. John Jr. was at the center of things like the hole in a doughnut, crying while the doctor and nurses went about their duties and his mother doted on him. His lungs proved his presence like a clarinet in a marching band. Strands of red hair and green eyes filled out the small face of the city's newest member. The hospital staff methodically checked him, and his mother watched protectively.

City noises—honking horns, ringing phones, the train passing down the tracks—all seemed in place. City sights—the white walls of the hospital, the budding trees outside, and the blue, blue sky—were the same as yesterday. City smells—the scent of the medicines, the fresh cotton garments, the humid air—all would have been noticed without the presence of John Argent Jr., but Mrs. Argent hugged her baby close to her chest and then held him up triumphantly as nurses passing down the hall peeked in and smiled. John Jr. stopped crying and quizzically eyed the scene, looking as if he were staking out his audience like an actor.

Outside was a big city. Minneapolis was an expanding city. Founded on the Mississippi River before the Civil War, Minneapolis was alive with action. It was largely a Scandinavian enclave, but other groups also resided within its relatively defined neighborhoods.

The time was 1955, and it was spring. Senator Hubert Humphrey topped the news with his criticism of President Dwight Eisenhower's Southeast Asian policy, but the weather was great. It was sixty degrees.

The next six years held no special memories.

In my first-grade class, the biggest impression I had was the praise and criticism I received for spending an inordinately long time on a project in class while the rest of the class waited for me to finish. Miss Goal said my work was excellent, but I shouldn't take up all the rest of the class's time to do it.

The next year, I sat on the floor and tried to listen to my second-grade teacher read a story to the class. She was a pretty woman with dark hair and fashionable glasses. I was unable to concentrate on what she was reading, as I found myself staring at her nylon stockings. They made me feel excited. The more I tried to listen, the more distracted I became. I wanted some answer, some response from the teacher, on my interest in her nylons, but she seemed unconcerned if not unaware of me. I picked up a small stone off the classroom floor and threw it at her legs.

"Someone's throwing something at my legs! It hurts. I want them to stop it right now!" Miss Williams said, not sounding as if she really expected to find out the culprit. I hid my head in shame and tried to turn my attention back to the story.

A year later, I sat at my desk at Hale Elementary School. I was in the third wooden desk from the front. Nathan Hale Elementary School was named after the patriot who regretted that he only had one life to live for his country. It was a solid, two-story, redbrick building in South Minneapolis. The name of the school was engraved in the mortar that was the trim between the floors. I sat at my desk with only my one life to live for the city.

Barbara Handsome, the prettiest girl in the class, sat one row over and to the front. Her self-conscious smile sent me into a dream. *If only I could get her attention*, I thought, *I'd be happy*. She didn't notice me too much. For one thing, I wasn't the best-looking boy in the class. I had red hair and freckles, which was generally despised by others and consequently by myself. Tim Wilson was the most attractive boy in the class. Barbara seemed more interested in him. Her blond hair bobbed gently as she looked up at the teacher and then around at the classroom.

I tried to concentrate on the teacher, Mrs. Johnson, an older woman in her sixties. Her eyes were lively, but I could sense sadness. It was as though there were tears in her soul. If she was sad, why didn't she talk about it? Up in front of the class, she sat reading, and I listened intently, trying to learn more. The other children squirmed in their seats, but Mrs. Johnson remained in firm control. I looked back and forth at Mrs. Johnson and Barbara Handsome.

At three o'clock, the bell rang, and we watched Mrs. Johnson as she told us we could leave. Jim Hoknoski, my best friend, walked up to me by the door.

"Do you want to play football today?" he asked.

"Okay, I'll see if my brother Fred wants to play too."

As we got out into the city air, I looked around at

all the children who were running, jumping, and yelling. I knew a lot of them by name. I looked over at Jim, my best friend, but I couldn't say that I really knew him or that he knew me.

"I'll talk to Fred when I get home, Jim."

"Okay, John."

I set my sights on my home, a stucco two-story house built in the 1930s. My father kept the yard looking perfect, and I was proud of our house. I thought the birch tree in the front yard was very cool. Once inside, my mother asked me how school went. I muttered a few things, and then I told her that I was going over to Jim's to play football. I asked if Fred was around.

"No," she said, "but Brett is." Brett was two years younger than I—too young for football with the older boys.

I walked nonchalantly past houses where other city people lived, all similar to the one I lived in. Our neighborhood was made up of middle-class families who took pride in our city. The homes were well kept up, and even the air smelled clean. The grass in the yards was green, but the trees had started to turn color into brilliant yellows and reds. I was in my shirtsleeves looking back at the sun that was four o'clock high. I was right on time.

I came to Jim's one-story stucco house that spread itself over most of the lot. A rather short woman wearing makeup and red lipstick opened the door.

"Hi, Mrs. Hoknoski. Is Jim here?"

"John, he'll be right there."

In a moment, Jim appeared in a T-shirt and jeans, carrying a football. His sandy hair came up to about my eye level.

"Where's Fred?" he quizzed me.

"Couldn't come, and Brett's too young," I responded.

"Maybe my brothers will play, or else we'll get some guys from around the block."

"Okay."

We played our game across from Jim's front yard in the vacant lot next door. There were trees in the way, and the ground was uneven. We tried hard, but we dropped passes left and right. Runs went for short yardage. Sometimes, a player would burst out in anger at a teammate over some failure.

"Jim! Why didn't you catch that one? What's wrong with you?"

"The sun was right in my eyes. I didn't see the ball coming."

"Okay, we'll try the same play again."

We didn't give up easily. We all were going to be high school stars. Next door to Jim lived a boy who was currently a three-letter varsity athlete. Sometimes he would come out when we were playing. We all tried harder then, and if he smiled, we felt warm inside.

After the game, Jim and I said good-bye, and I headed for home. When I got there, I called Jim to make sure everything was okay.

"Hi, Jim. How are you?"

"Good. How about you?"

"See you tomorrow in school?"

"Yeah."

"Okay."

My mother came into the room. "Didn't you just get done playing football with Jim?" she asked.

"Yeah."

"And you're calling him right away again?"

"Oh, Mom."

I walked into the living room and turned on the TV.

"Get ready for supper, John. Your father will be home soon."

My mom was a pretty-looking woman in her midthirties with very expressive eyes, raised on a farm in western Minnesota but well adapted to the city. She had three square meals on the table every day, knew what her children were doing most of the time, and was a loving wife for my dad. Committed to liberal thinking, she gave her children a certain degree of freedom to make their own mistakes.

The next day at school, Mrs. Johnson called on me to answer a question.

I had been looking around the room at the other students. I didn't know the answer.

"John, what's wrong? Don't you know the answer to my question?"

"I'm sorry." I stared blankly at my desktop until she called on someone else. I felt a pit in my stomach.

After school, Jim and I walked home together.

"What was wrong with you today, John?"

"Nothing. I didn't know the answer. That's all."

"You want to play football today?"

"Sure."

I looked around at the houses. On each city block, there were twelve of them, standing lots that were 50 feet wide and 110 feet long. Most of them were stucco, and a few of them built out of wood. I identified the homes of fellow students, and they were of interest to me. The rest were just property.

When I got home, my parents weren't there. My mom had left a note.

> *John,*
> *Your father and I and your brothers are*
> *out shopping.*

We will be home at 5:30.
Love, Mom

I had the whole house to myself; what a chance for temptation. On impulse, I walked into my parents' bedroom, not my usual territory, and I went to the drawer where my mother kept her nylon stockings. I grabbed a pair and rubbed them in my hands, their silkiness and sheerness giving me quite a thrill.

I had a pang of guilt, but I couldn't help myself. I knew it was wrong, yet I did it. Then I remembered the reaction of my second-grade teacher and wondered what my mother would say if she knew.

When I heard the garage door opening, I quickly put the stockings back in the drawer and ran out of the bedroom, meeting my parents just as they were coming through the door.

"Hi, John," said Dad.

"John, have you been home long?" Mom asked.

"I got home at 5:00," I said. "I was over at Jim's."

"Why don't you go practice the piano while I get dinner ready?" said Mom.

My piano lesson would take a half hour, and I would see the teacher in two days.

"Do I have to do that now?" I asked.

"Yes, John. You have to be ready when Mr. Samuels comes. You're not ready yet, are you?"

"No."

The piano was an old upright that had once been at my grandparents' house, a couple of miles northeast of us. My mother had learned to play beautifully. Now I sat on the stool banging away, often looking over my shoulder out the window.

"Suppertime."

I thought I'd never heard such pleasant words.

We said grace and began passing food.

"Fred, how did school go today?" Dad asked.

Fred was a fifth grader. He was always in the top of his class.

"Oh, fine," he said.

"What are you working on?"

"Minnesota history, multiplication and division, experiments with animals, and singing."

"How about you, John?"

"Penmanship, reading, arithmetic, and singing."

"Brett, how is school going for you?"

"Fine."

"What are you working on?"

"Drawing and reading."

My mother sat watching intently. Soon dinner was over, and my brothers and I turned on the TV.

"I want to watch *Caveman*," I said, jumping toward the TV.

"No, wrestling," said Fred, quickly grabbing me by the arm.

"No, let's watch *Happy Island*," said Brett, trying to squeeze between us.

My father came into the living room to find out what the arguing was all about.

"Can't you work something out?" he asked.

"Brett had his choice last night," Fred said.

"Fred always gets his choice," said Brett.

"I never get my choice," I said.

"How do you ever expect to get along in the city with others if you can't work your problems out with your brothers at home?"

"Okay. We'll all take turns," said Fred.

"You take your pick now, Brett," I suggested. "I'll take mine at 7:00, and Fred can pick at 7:30."

"Now that is how you work things out," said Dad.

He was a man of average build with red hair just like mine. He had fought in the Battle of the Bulge in World War II, and his twin brother had been lost in the war. Dad had been kind of a big wheel at his college and now was a very popular teacher at a city high school.

He was a very busy man, but he did take the time to participate in a father-son group in the neighborhood with me. We called ourselves Indian guides. We rotated homes and hosts from week to week with one week being crafts, another sports, another taking in a movie, and any other activities a third grader and his father could participate in.

Jim and his dad were in the group. Jim's dad was a restaurateur. He was balding, but he made a lot of jokes about it.

On one outing, we went to a movie called *Old Yeller*, the story of a boy and his dog. The ending was sad.

"What did you think of the movie?" asked Mr. Hoknoski as we came out of the theater.

"It was kind of sad," I said, almost beginning to cry.

"Poor dog. Probably better off in heaven, if dogs make it there," he said with a laugh.

"Yeah, I guess it wasn't so bad." I smiled.

Jim and I were also in another activity at a local church. Although I had gone to church with my parents for as long as I could remember, I had a unique experience one night.

A minister came up to me after the meeting and sort of directed me over to a wall. It kind of threatened me.

"John, I have a big question for you tonight."

"You do?"

"Have you ever let Jesus into your heart?"

"Well, I go to church."

"That's not what I mean."

"What, then?"

"I want you to look at me and say, 'Lord, I accept you as my savior.'"

"Lord, I accept you as my savior."

I felt a kind of warmth in my heart. I looked up at him and asked if I had done it right.

"Go now. You've just made the biggest choice of your life."

It felt otherworldly to me, like it was a foreign experience from the city.

It was several weeks later that we got the tragic news. President Kennedy had been assassinated. I was in school at the time, and we all looked around in shock. We must have assumed that the president was invincible. How could God let that happen? Mrs. Johnson dismissed class.

"Mom, did you hear the bad news?" I asked, coming through the door.

"Oh, John, it's terrible," she said. "It's as though the whole world ended."

I remembered how Mr. Hoknoski had eased my sorrow with a joke a few months earlier: "Probably better off in heaven."

"John, how could you say such a stupid thing?"

Humor didn't always work. I looked at my mom and knew it was really sad.

The TV coverage lasted well over a week. Everyone in the city was mourning. I felt empty, stunned. How could such a great man be brought down by a fanatic? If President Kennedy was vulnerable, who wasn't? I must be too. I prayed to the Lord for help. The only thing that seemed permanent was God.

I was being thrust into the city, but it wasn't necessarily permanent. With the Cold War going on, we could be blown off the map at any time. Who could help me with this?

2

MRS. MULCHIN, MY fourth-grade teacher, was a precious woman. Her heart-shaped face bespoke the kindness in her personality. She had genuine concern for all her students. She was older like Mrs. Johnson, and she didn't give me the physical sensation that Miss Williams had. She was more like a combination of a mother and grandmother.

"Class, today I will be reading from *Huckleberry Finn*. Does anyone know who wrote that?"

I raised my hand, as did some of the others.

"John?"

"Mark Twain."

"Very good, John. Mark Twain was known for his wit and his social commentary. He has been criticized for his portrayal of blacks with the character of Jim. However, in his day, there was a lot more racial prejudice out in the open. It was a different era. If we understand that, we can still see the book as a great gift to literature. Mark Twain placed a notice in the book, saying, 'Persons attempting to find a motive in this narrative will be prosecuted; persons attempting to find a moral in it will be banished; persons attempting to find a plot in it will be shot.' Can you see how Twain was offering up this work for reading pleasure only? Therefore, we might be able to take something serious like racial prejudice and forget its ill effects. We can still enjoy the work as a whole. Our lives are like that. If we become too serious, we really lose the value of what is offered."

That was really an intelligent way to look at life, I thought.

On the way home from school with Jim, we had a conversation.

"Do you like Mrs. Mulchin?" I asked Jim.

"Yeah, she's okay."

"She seems to really care about the students."

"I'm glad I got in her class."

"She was funny when she was reading us that book."

"Yeah, she is pretty cool."

"I wonder what Barbara Handsome thinks of her."

"What does that have to do with anything?"

"Don't you think Barbara is kind of cute?"

"She wouldn't have anything to do with us."

"Don't you think so?"

"Nope. She likes Tim Wilson."

"What's he got that we don't?"

"Good looks."

"His hair looks like a chocolate candy bar."

I remembered when I had been really sad that people made fun of my hair. Mrs. Mulchin had complimented my hair. My dad had always told me to tease back people who teased me.

When I got home, Fred was practicing the trombone.

"Hey, Johnny baby. How's it going?"

"That noise hurts my ears."

"Is that a banana between your eyes?"

"Why? Are you a hungry monkey?"

"Boys!" My mother came into the room. "Fred, you're supposed to be practicing. John, you go help your father rake leaves."

"Doesn't Brett have to do anything?" I asked.

"He's younger. He's not as strong as you."

Our yard consisted of a small patch of grass in the back, a strip of grass along one side of the house, and a roomier space in front. My dad was almost done raking.

"Dad, Mom sent me out to help you rake."

"That's okay, John. I'm just about done. Here's a

quarter. Go buy yourself a candy bar at the store before dinner."

"What will Mom say?"

"You don't have to tell her."

I could always count on my dad in a pinch.

I walked over to Hanesworth Pharmacy.

"Hi, John," May the clerk said.

"Hi."

A Double Whack chocolate bar was twenty-five cents.

"That will spoil your dinner!" exclaimed May.

I just smiled and left. I tore the wrapper off and threw it on the ground. The chocolate was sweet. I loved to let it melt in my mouth before I swallowed it. When I got home, it was dinnertime. I ate everything even though it wasn't easy.

"John, you didn't miss a bite. Your teacher would be proud."

"Thanks, Mom."

"We'll have to invite your teacher over to see this sometime," said my dad.

"Dad, you're not funny," I returned.

"Are you going to do your homework now?" my mother questioned me.

"Can't I watch TV?" I begged.

"John, we've been through this before."

"Just for a half hour."

"*John.*"

"Okay, you win, but when I become the president of the United States, I'll make a law against homework."

"There you go, John, but for now, you'll have to listen to your mother," entered my father.

"Okay," I responded. I grabbed my books and went out to the dining room table. Fred was in the adjoining living room watching TV.

"Ha-ha. Johnny's doing his homework," laughed Fred.

"Someone has got to be the brains in the family," I said.

Fred sat on the blue sofa watching a twenty-four-inch black and white. His brown hair was cut so he had bangs just over his eyebrows. It was a Beatles haircut, the same as mine.

"What are you watching, anyway, Fred?"

"John, are you going to be able to do your homework or not?" asked my mother, coming into the dining room.

"Okay, Mom. Fred, stop talking to me."

"John, if you're ever going to become an adult, you'll have to take responsibility for your own life."

"Mom, I'm nine years old. What do you expect?"

"Don't your teachers show you how to act?"

"Yeah, okay, Mom. Okay."

I opened my arithmetic book and began to study. *I suppose I've got to get these problems done,* I thought. *Mrs. Mulchin won't like it if I don't have my homework ready. Then she'll tell my parents at conference time. Mom and Dad won't let me do anything fun then. If I get done fast, maybe I'll have time to call Jim yet tonight. I can't wait until I get old enough to be an adult. They're cool. They get to do what they want when they want to. Everyone tells kids what to do. Nobody leaves us alone. There are people around all the time. Half of them don't like you. They just order you about. They don't care. I try to be a nice guy. I think Jim likes me. Maybe he's the only one. My parents just boss me around. I don't think they love me. I don't think Barbara Handsome likes me, either. I'm too ugly. With my red hair, who'd want me?*

"John, are you concentrating on your homework?" asked my mom as she came back into the dining room.

The wooden chair creaked as I leaned back.

"Don't do that."

"What?"

"Leaning back on the chair."

"Mom, can I go downtown tomorrow with Jim?"

"No. You're only nine years old. You can't expect to do things adults can."

"Why?"

"You just can't."

Adults get to do everything. Kids can't do anything. It's not fair.

"Mom, I'm done with homework. Can I watch TV with Fred?"

"Are you sure you're done? Let me see."

"We had twenty problems in arithmetic. See? All done."

"Okay, John. You can watch for one hour, but then it's to bed."

"Okay, Mom."

Time passed.

On December 9, 1964, we had our first heavy snowfall, ten inches. I was silly enough to enjoy the stuff. Most of the adults complained about the snow. As a city boy, I looked upon snow as an adventure. I would trek across people's yards just to leave my footprints. When I was done, I'd look back proudly as if I had left some kind of legacy. I made snowballs too, and I threw them at everything in sight, including trees, signs, and people I knew. With the snow came cold. The adults talked about the wind blowing right through them. I didn't feel that way. Even on the coldest of days, I always felt a warmth within. Perhaps it was God in my heart. Perhaps it was also that my parents always made sure that I had warm clothes.

"Okay, children, class will begin," said Mrs. Mulchin as the bell rang. "The principal will soon be on the intercom. We'll wait for her message."

Within thirty seconds, *bing, bing, bong.* "This is Justin Stop, your principal. I hope you're having a good day. There's some snow on the ground. We want you all to be careful. It's very slippery. Cars can skid out of control, so keep your eyes wide open when crossing the street. You are all precious children, and I wouldn't want to see any of you get hurt. Your parents love you. We all want you to be careful." *Bing, bing, bong.*

"Principal Stop wants you all to be careful, students. If we're all careful, we will all have long, useful lives," Mrs. Mulchin theorized. Her purple dress was balanced by a white pearl necklace. Her hair was always so well groomed. When she smiled, it wasn't a silly grin but a knowing, caring, slow smile. Then it broadened with a reassurance that something kind would be said.

"Betty Wood, why don't you come up to the blackboard and do the first five problems of the arithmetic assignment? You always do such a good job."

Betty was one of the smartest people in class. She was always attentive to the teacher, and the rest of the kids almost seemed to be in her shadow. She was so proud as she strolled up to the board. With great authority for a nine-year-old, she took up the chalk and wrote out the answers. She got them all right. The rest of us kind of sheepishly grinned.

What makes her think she's so good? She's not as pretty as Barbara Handsome. Maybe her mom helped her with the homework. No, she probably did it herself. Why does she have to be such a showoff?

After school, Jim and I walked home as usual. All around us, city kids frolicked as they found their way home. At this time of year, they all wore winter coats, gloves or mittens, and boots. It was probably thirty degrees, but the smiles on everyone's faces were as fresh as spring. Children were going home where they would be greeted by concerned parents. There was reason for joy.

The two of us strode along with other students who were in pairs ten feet in front of us and ten feet in back and so on. It looked something like the line for Noah's ark. Adults drove by in cars. Some of them looked out their windows. Others hardly gave us the least bit of attention.

I was always looking for clues. What was the city about? Where did I fit in? Was I doing the right thing? A smile from an adult could give me the self-satisfaction and security I needed. Mrs. Mulchin had the quality I sought. How about Barbara Handsome? And what about this desire I had for women's nylons? Maybe I should try to be smart like Betty Wood.

"Do you want to come over and shoot pool in my basement?" Jim asked.

"No, I'd better go home," I said. "My mom is expecting me."

I was lying. I knew my parents and brothers were going to be gone. When I got home, I went into my mother's drawer and took out a pair of nylons. I undressed. For the first time ever, I put on one and then the other. It aroused me immensely. I felt that I was in sheer ecstasy. I looked at myself in the mirror. *A naughty boy*, I thought. I might have kept them on for hours, but I didn't want to take the chance of getting caught. Carefully, I took them off and put them back in the drawer. Then I put my pants back on and went out into the kitchen to get something to eat.

My parents and brothers will be home soon, I thought. *The snow looks so cold outside. I wonder if I should go out. No, I'll stay inside. It's warm in here. Too cold out there. There's nothing to do. Maybe I'll go watch TV.*

"Okay, masked man, your time is up."

"Not so quick, you scum. What's behind you?"

"Uff."

Whap, whap.

"Now I'll take you somewhere where you belong."

I was glad the good guy won. I hated bad guys.

I could hear the garage door opening and the sound of the car driving in.

"Hi, Mom. Where have you been?" I questioned.

"With your brothers out Christmas shopping."

"Did you buy me something I can't use?" I quipped.

"We're not telling you anything," returned Fred.

"When are you going to do your shopping?" asked my mother.

"When can you take me?"

"Plan ahead. Make a list. These things don't just happen."

"I know, Mom. I know."

"When you get ready, let me know."

"Fred, what do you want? A rock?"

"I bought you a hairnet," said Brett.

"Boys! Boys!" Our mom never liked to see us tease each other.

Our dad was a tease, though. He would call us girls sometimes. Other times, he would rhyme our names with nonsensical words—*John the pond* and so on. The way I heard it, he was always a tease. My aunts had clued me in on that. His two sisters told us everything about him. I always thought it was okay that my father had a sense of humor.

He was usually funny except when one of the boys did something wrong. Then he could get quite angry—almost out of control. It was because he wanted us to do the right thing. Both of my parents encouraged conscientious behavior. If we did the right thing, we were rewarded. I wanted to do the right thing in the city.

In school, Mrs. Mulchin usually congenially greeted our class. However, on January 2, 1965, she wasn't her pleasant self. We quickly found out why.

"Somebody tried to snatch my purse last night when I was out for a walk!" she exclaimed. "Let this be a lesson to you all. There are some people who you cannot trust. Minneapolis can be a tough place sometimes."

Don Jacobs, one of the boys in class, raised a smirk on his face.

"Don, I don't for the life of me see what is funny here," Mrs. Mulchin scorched.

The rest of the class sat on the edge of their seats in wonderment. What would Don say?

"No, it's not funny. I'm sorry."

Mrs. Mulchin sure told him. I guess he should be sorry. There's nothing funny about having your purse snatched. I wonder what he'd think if someone grabbed for his wallet. No, that's not funny at all.

"Children—and Don, you especially—I don't want any of you to end up like that boy downtown. He's got a terrible thing to deal with on his conscience. Imagine the situation he's in. You should all be glad that you're a lot better off than he is. Now we can begin our class." From angry to sweet, Mrs. Mulchin started with our lessons.

How can she change her emotions so quickly? One second she's so stern, the next second she's so nice.

"Does anyone know who Ben Franklin was and how he discovered electricity?"

And so it went, questions and answers. If you got the answer right, most of the people in class approved. For that moment, you were a star. The city was the world, and most of us wanted to be a part of it. If Mrs. Mulchin kept feeding us questions and we kept delivering responses, we would become part of the city. Although we may not have had a lot of choice, most of us seemed satisfied with the process. We may not have understood it then. I can only begin to understand it now as I look back to that time.

After the parent conferences, my parents came home with a favorable report on my progress in fourth grade from Mrs. Mulchin.

"John, I'm proud of you," said my mother as she came through the front door.

"Hi, Mom."

"Yes, John," said my father. "Your work in school is good. That's what we ask of you—that you do well in school. Good work in school should carry you through life."

Life was the city. It was the buildings downtown, the people, and the houses. I had no way of relating to all this at once, but somehow I thought that someday I would. Maybe school was the answer. I had no way of knowing. I trusted my parents on that one.

The phone rang.

"John, it's for you," called my mother.

"Hello?"

"It's Jim."

"Hi."

"What did Mrs. Mulchin say about you to your parents?"

"I got good news."

"You did?"

"Didn't you?"

"Well . . . okay, I guess."

"What's wrong?"

"Mrs. Mulchin told my parents I was just average."

"Oh, that's too bad."

"See you tomorrow."

I felt bad for Jim. I guess I wanted everyone to be in the top group like I was. That wasn't possible, so I just tried to sympathize. It was one of my unwritten rules that when a city boy who was my friend was feeling down, I tried to help out the best I could. A lot of other city boys and city girls were beyond my thoughts, but there could be one or two that I didn't get along with. Sometimes I was the bully; other times, I was bullied.

Jackson McVane was a weird-looking kid. He had curly hair, thick glasses, and a flat nose. In class, Jackson would always get the answer wrong. After class, city boys picked on him. Occasionally, I would join in. It usually involved a little pushing and shoving as well as name taunts. Jackson would eventually get away looking quite shaken. I thought if we just shook him up enough, he'd become normal.

Glenn Olson was a stocky city boy, the kind who played football for the park board. He was my bully. Glenn would catch me on the streets and shake me down for money or candy—whatever I had.

I always felt Glenn would be punished by God. I never figured I would be punished for what I did to Jackson.

The city was on my side, I thought. I wasn't able to entertain another's perspective. It must have been the love of God that made me think that. How else could I have seen everything so one sided? It didn't occur to me that if God loved me, I should love others and love God. I didn't know how.

3

"JIM, ARE WE going to play pompom pull-away or kickball?"

We were at recess, and it was a sixty-degree day in April.

"We only have fifteen minutes."

"It hardly matters what we do."

"What do you want to do?"

"Kick myself in the head."

"What?"

"Put my underwear up the flagpole."

"Come on, get serious."

"Serious? What's there to get serious about?"

"John, let's go play kickball."

"Okay, Jim."

Back in class, Mrs. Mulchin stood in front of us like an actress in a play.

"Now, children, you have had your share of fun for the day. It's time to dig in."

The only thing serious is the city. She's just up there because she has to be. She might care about us, but what good does that do? I want to play outside some more.

"Children, you should all get to know some of the cities and towns in Minnesota. Does anyone know the population of Minnesota?"

Betty Wood raised her hand.

What does it matter? Big deal if she knows.

When I got home from school, my mom met me in the living room. Our house was a two-story, four-bedroom home. It was just the right size to hold three boys and my parents. In the living room, we had a couch and two chairs. We also had a rocking chair that once belonged to Grannie, my father's mother. There were a couple of lamps, a black-and-white TV, and a painting on one wall.

"How'd school go today?"

"Okay, Mom. Okay."

"Are you ready for your piano lesson this week?"

"Jim and I were going to play catch."

"John, you know how I feel about putting sports ahead of your piano."

"Yeah, but the guys will think I'm a sissy or something."

"There's nothing sissyish about the piano."

"Mom, I'm a city boy, not a city girl."

"I know you're a boy."

"Boys are supposed to play sports."

"Whoever told you that?"

"Dad."

Dad wants me to play sports. This idea of the piano is all my mother's. She must think I'm a girl or something. I wouldn't mind being a good piano player, but I should be playing sports. I should be more like a city boy.

"Mom, why can't I go play ball with Jim?"

"Okay, John. I don't want to force you to do something you don't want to, but remember, there's nothing wrong with playing piano. A lot of great men were piano players."

I grabbed my mitt from the back porch, opened the screen door, and went down the back steps. As I passed a man on the sidewalk, I socked my mitt a couple of times with my free hand. The man smiled his approval. Jim was out in his yard waiting.

"Jim, I'm lucky my mom let me come over."

"Why?"

"She wanted me to practice the piano."

"What fun is that?"

"I know."

"Boy, your parents have got some weird ideas."

I love my mom, but she's goofed up. I can't cope with it. I want to have fun, but she just wants to boss me around. Jim is fun.

"Jim, go over there so I can throw you the ball."

"Why don't you?"

"Let's not argue over something stupid."

"Then you go over there."

"Okay."

Jim can be fun. Sometimes he's bossy too. Why can't people just be nice?

"Okay, toss it to me."

"You dropped it."

"I wasn't trying."

"You goof."

"A goof? Isn't that something like a doof?"

"You're that too."

"If I want insults, I'll look at your face."

"Least I'm not a freckle-face strawberry."

"Here, see if you can catch this one."

It was the simple pleasures in life that captivated us. Time has a way of bringing up into the forefront the things that were important in my life. I remember when I was ten. Jim was a good friend. His friendship was my start on the road to being a city boy. At that point, there was not much more required than residence to be one.

However, the rules would get tougher. One hardship arose in my relationship with Jim.

The school year was almost over. It was June 10, 1965. As I arrived at school, Jim walked up to me outside the building.

"John, I have some bad news."

"You are bad news."

"No, I mean it."

"What could be so bad, Jim?"

"This year will be my last in Minneapolis."

"What?"

"We're moving to Texas."

"Oh, yeah?"

I must remain calm. This can't be happening, but it is happening. What am I going to do without my best friend? At least act like you're concerned about him.

"When are you leaving, Jim?"

"End of June."

"We'll have to have a big party for you."

"Whatever you want to do."

The bell rang, so we had to get inside.

That summer at the time Jim left, I could feel a piece of me leaving with him. It was like getting a flat tire on your bike or having your pet die. You'd survive, but you didn't feel that hot. Something inside gnawed at you. I guess it must have been Jim's spirit placing itself into a new setting.

Even at my early age, I turned to God for answers. I knew God would replace the loss I felt. It would take time.

Time is all a jumbled process for me now. Thinking back from 1990 to 1965, some things that happened yesterday seem longer ago than Jim moving. Perhaps it is the depth of the loss. Those things that hurt exist with clarity forever. Shakespeare said time heals all wounds. It is truer that time deals with all wounds. Sometimes the hurt can grow.

In this case, my wounds would heal. I was a city boy. Losing a friend was part of city life. It was something I had to accept. It could even make me a stronger person. Loss could do that. Some people thrive on their own adversity. I wanted to be one of those.

"Mom, Jim's family is moving away from Minneapolis!" I exclaimed to her when she greeted me at the door.

"Oh, John. That's terrible."

"It could be worse."

"How?"

"The Russians could have invaded."

"John, I don't know how you can joke about something serious."

"Laughter is the food for life."

I took pride in having a good sense of humor. Laughing would become my second nature. I would always begin a relationship by seeking a smile. Oftentimes, I would have someone I barely knew in stitches within moments.

Tom People moved into the neighborhood that summer after I finished fourth grade. He was a tall and filled-out city boy—a football player. Another city boy, David Leaf, introduced me to Tom. I wasn't very familiar with David, so my introduction to Tom was shaky at best.

"Tom, this is John Argent."

"Nerdy redhead," commented Tom.

"I just use this hair color in the summer," I jested.

Tom liked the joke, and we became instant friends. The element of truth in my statement was there. My hair became redder in the summer. It was also self-effacing and eased any awkward tension. The main thing I think Tom liked, though, is that it was gutsy. It showed nerve. I felt with a statement like that I would either win or lose. I had won. It didn't hurt that David nodded his approval.

"Glad to know you, John," said Tom.

"Thanks."

"Do you live around here?"

"I live just down the block from David."

"You gonna be on the football team in the fall?"

"I don't know yet."

"What's the matter, you chicken?"

See what I mean about the challenges getting tougher? What would these guys think if they knew I had worn my mother's nylons? I shuddered to imagine.

"No, I'm not chicken. I just haven't decided yet."

"You're a little small."

"Leave John alone," entered David.

"I'm just giving the guy a hard time," returned Tom.

"It's all right," I said diplomatically.

I was just starting to realize that in the city, using tact could go a long way. A little kindness might not be easy, but digging down to summon it up was worth it. It was the Christian answer. Christ rarely got angry. For the most part, he was very easygoing, and he avoided bickering. When he did get angry, he was sure that he was right. I didn't feel like reacting with anger to a little teasing. I also wasn't sure I was right in the first place by trying to be with Tom and David. It did seem like they were concerned mostly about themselves. I felt that if anyone got in their way, that person would be ostracized. I had usually been concerned about others. Nonetheless, I figured I'd humor them and get along that way. They did seem a little exciting to be around.

The sun shone down with some heat on the mi-dafternoon day. The grass had turned green, and the leaves were out on the trees. City folks were all about. A couple of them were mowing their yards. Some were walking their dogs. Others waited for the bus.

Tom, David, and I kept walking.

"So are you an A student?" asked Tom.

"They don't give grades in school at this age," I said.

"You've got an answer for everything," mocked Tom.

"John is one of the smartest guys in class," interjected David.

"Yeah, right," I said. I certainly didn't know how smart I was, but it would be my way to try to think through the city.

4

THE CITY WAS willing to bestow acceptance upon me as I grew. I could tell the difference between acceptance and rejection. This is because my life was moving, and I could recognize subtleties. Rejection felt like heat in the summer; acceptance was like a drink of water from a spring well. Acceptance did me well.

In a way, I thought the city's extension of acceptance for me was due to something I did. I thought it was my sense of humor or my good intentions. I must say that even though I goofed off, I still had desire to do right. It seemed like people knew that just by looking at me. Even people in cars on the street seemed to know. I must have been accepted because I deserved it, I felt. Being accepted by the city was fine. I couldn't always get acceptance from people, but the city would take stock in me.

I didn't exactly trust everything about the Twin Cities; I had a wait-and-see attitude. Maybe in a while, my parents would allow me to go places. For now, I just had to accept city life as it was just as the city had accepted me. At night, I would lie on my bed under the covers and peep out knowing that for miles around me was the city. I was surrounded by it. This is just the way it was. I was a kid at sea on dry land.

My life was really in a tumult, but I didn't think all that much about it. Maybe I had problems with girls. I focused on what I could expect to happen next in my life. I was service oriented. By that, I mean I wasn't on an ego trip; I was dedicated to humanity. I was too young to do much; however, I had all the feelings of a martyr. No one realized I was so spilt in myself that I couldn't get needs met and that I resorted to principles and ideals to make my life make sense. What sense I could make was little. I didn't understand the purpose, so I goofed off. I had high ideals with limited behavior in that direction. I went to church and school, but only because I had to. I was interested really in going downtown or anywhere just to move like everyone else. My nature was sedate as long as I could keep moving. I had just about given up on claiming what I really wanted in life. Maybe I didn't know what I wanted. I liked girls, but I was too young. Sometimes I felt as though the world was too crazy. I wanted to get out of the world and get to heaven; that would be ideal. I was growing more and more into something I didn't like. I was becoming a person I didn't respect.

I survived by building friendships. I met a lot of people, but no one could replace Jim, so I began to give up on something like understanding from others. I formed friendships that were based on being cool and having a good image. My image became me instead of the true me. It's that so much was going on all the time one had to be a bit of an actor to keep functioning. The act I chose gave me at least a way of dealing with people. I was nice to everyone whether I liked them or not, and I tried to simulate coolness. Coolness was an answer to the hardships and otherwise unanswerable questions that surfaced in a city. If I could just remain cool or become cool, I would be elated. Coolness was a road to happiness. It wasn't easy to be cool, though, for different reasons. However, it was the direction to go. The city challenged coolness, but my friends were there. Even if the city rubbed us wrong, we were not upset. Any friction was sanded off, like wood with sandpaper. The surface of life was smooth. I drank in what was around me even when it wasn't pleasant. My eyes fastened onto an image, and it was an answer to my questions about what to do with my life. I was to be a servant to people. I was an outsider—a misfit—except I had more and more friends. God must have been guiding my life. The harder I tried to screw it up, the more good things happened. Friends were an excellent example. I don't know how, but I had a lot of friends. I was together enough not to say stupid things. I was also service oriented even with my friends so that I was more giving than taking. I didn't impose undue hardship upon the relationships. My needs were subordinate to the friendship. The relationship was elevated by not concentrating on what I was going to get out of it.

I also had a sense of adventure. Whether it was smoking cigarettes or ringing doorbells or thieving apples, I would do it all. I didn't care. It wasn't wrong to me, because in my heart it felt right. It felt good, and that was the justification. It wasn't just the pleasure; I felt opposed to a lot of the values of adults. They seemed so narrow-minded; I had become wide open—or at least I thought so. I had opened to a situation in which I had a maximum interaction with people. I became in tune with a variety of personalities. I didn't stop people when they were saying something to me. It always seemed to lead toward the edge that one lived on in a city. People told me their secrets, removing barriers that would have made the edge dull. In my case, the edge was sharp. The edge was the culmination of desire and effort. It arose out of people's lives like a rainbow arises out of a storm to give people a sighting of life. The edge divided up the goals and personalities, such as a classroom or a city, giving people an opportunity to interact from a sharp focus. As children, the edge was partly ours and partly made by adults. We the kids were foremost students. That is what the adults created for us. As kids, however, we saw differences among us, and we created some of the edge ourselves. Some kids were cool, others were responsible, and others were trouble-makers. The edge was formed taking into account all factors. The edge gave me strength to carry on even though a lot of me was in turmoil and far from sharp. If I could stay in tune with the edge, I would be all right. Minneapolis was kind of like Disneyland—that is, life happened like you were watching a movie. It seemed only partly real. Friends were coming and going, moments made impressions sometimes while it was not really clear why, and a person felt a little bit apart from it all. I felt like the ball was rolling as I tried to figure which direction it would go. After being turned around enough times, I settled into an act that was contrary to recognized status quo. I changed a lot. I was growing, rebelling, and goofing off. The only thing permanent seemed to be laughter.

I liked to have people laugh with me. If they laughed at me, it was a different matter, but that didn't happen.

I'm ashamed to admit I did laugh at others, especially Miss Downfall, my fifth-grade teacher. She seemed to be such a stake in the ground. It's as though she could not roll with the humor. In my youth, I couldn't understand someone who could not laugh. It seemed tragic. I recoiled like a baby from touching a hot stove. I couldn't comprehend adults like Miss Downfall. I felt she knew I was okay.

When we would laugh in her class, she would stand there, her auburn hair shining, her face aghast, and her blackbird eyes pecking the air as she decided how to handle us. She seemed to understand us. She wasn't too ruffled, but she would warn us we were going to get in trouble.

It didn't seem like trouble to me. The city would always be there; I always had that. She was just a teacher who I didn't agree with. I liked music and laughter and sports. My sense of excitement had nothing to do with school. I was waiting for the day when I could be like an adult and go where I pleased in the city. That was living. It wasn't as Miss Downfall had it; I was headed for fun, not trouble.

To spur me on, I got a new baby brother, Keith.

5

MY SIXTH-GRADE TEACHER, Mrs. Never, made sure I wasn't going to cause any trouble in her class. She brought me into the cloakroom the first time I cut up, the very first day.

"You're not going to do that to me," said Mrs. Never.

"Do what?" I tried to ask.

"I know what you did to Miss Downfall last year," said Mrs. Never.

"Yeah," I mumbled.

"You're not going to do that to me," she reiterated. I knew I was going to have to experience the city outside of the classroom that year. I couldn't have those kinds of restrictions placed on me, a city boy.

It worked out, because I got my parents' approval to go downtown with my friends. I didn't need to seek city life in Mrs. Never's class. I'd go to class, but it wouldn't be important. I could go downtown now— that was important. It was like getting ready for a new level of finding the city.

On one hand, it wasn't a big deal; however, on the other side, it was a lot to me. Now I could see how adults were in their shiniest environment. I could explore the stores. I could be part of the full city. No longer penned into a small neighborhood, I was now taking man-size steps into the thick of my environment.

It was Saturday and a nice yellow, sunny, warm fall day. David Leaf, Tom People, and I got on a bus to head to the center of the city. We were going there so David could buy a football helmet for our team that I had also joined.

"Ten cents, boys," said the older bus driver.

I must have been all smiles, because he looked at me and said, "I don't see why you think that's so funny, Red." I stopped, looked, and then sat down. I guess it wasn't funny. Downtown could be a serious thing.

If my neighborhood was a beach ball, then downtown was an Olympic-size swimming pool. If my parents occasionally got ice cream as children during the Depression, then we got the privilege to go downtown. There was something focal about it. Not only was it the center of the city, it also stood up with tall buildings and catered to luxurious instincts with a decorative Nicollet Mall.

We three boys were not sophisticated downtowners, though, and we had a lot to learn. David, Tom, and I were too amazed at everything to pass as sophisticated. We were amateurs. The classy people strode down the mall as if they were all alone and owned it. Their eyes focused down the avenue, and they wore slight hints of smiles showing they knew something we didn't. It was complex.

Here were the three of us adjusting to this new part of the city, and we were out of place. I felt out of place, anyway. We stumbled around looking for a sporting goods store, but really we were just soaking in the sights of downtown.

My aim was not all that good. Since I had left the major confusion of early grade school to follow a direction that was a mixture of self-sacrifice and nonconformity, I was never able to really zone in on what I wanted. I ambulated. I didn't walk.

Downtown was like an event in my experiences; it wasn't shopping, really. My experience with my friends downtown was a formative adventure. I knew what it was like now to be at the hub of the city. There was a lot of movement, and there was gaiety and aloofness.

There was also a seediness that both enticed me and grabbed me. An old man with a brown bag passed by on the street. I was interested. It seemed like he could really tell a_story in the proper place. I felt so squeaky clean. I wanted to show him I cared. The man represented what could happen in a city. I wasn't overly full of compassion in the way of feeling sorry for him; I was moved more in the direction of amazement. To me, it was amazing that this man could get by with so little in the external world. I caught him looking at me, and I smiled. He wasn't unfriendly, but he looked rough. In a sense, he looked free, but how could he be? I didn't understand his chains to alcohol. I just figured he had had a hard life. Why would the city do that to him? I was trying to view him in the right way. My two friends didn't really note my preoccupation with the old man. It all happened quickly. I felt like I was taking it all in. In that man, I had seen a good part of the city. That was what I had come downtown for, really. I loved experiences. I could live vicariously through a man's life like his. He interested me more than any of the well-dressed people. At the same time, I felt like there was something I'd never know about him, and I would never be able to see in him the element of the city I was tuned in to. He would probably never know I existed.

That's how it could get in the city. There were just so many people who would never touch lives with me the way I imagined when I was younger. I had hopes of being well known in this city, but my vision was loose and far away. It wasn't a vision I could come to focus on. People like the old man were relegated to a position of suspension in the air as if I had no solution for them. I just didn't know what to do with the experience at the time. I couldn't achieve clarity on it.

Maybe I didn't want to. I just wanted downtown to be a fun spot for me. I wanted to learn about it, and I wanted to get a reaction from it. In a sense, I wanted a response from the city. The response I had gotten from the old man, his smile, was maybe enough. It was a touching smile.

We got to the store, bought a helmet, and took the bus home.

Things became less and less sober the older I got. I decided I wasn't going to be confused like when I was younger. I was making friends, staying busy, and getting into the order of things. I was a sixth grader. I was a young man and was taking on responsibility and getting respect. I was achieving a degree of independence. I was becoming aware of girls. I was having fun and learning about life.

The city was my home. Now that I could go downtown without supervision, I felt like a citizen. People in the city interested me, because they all had a kind of metropolitan look in their eyes. I saw it everywhere, just like in the eye of that old alcoholic. Behind the surface lay stories and deep mysteries and joy. Behind the eyes lay the secrets of every soul.

I was trying to understand how I was going to achieve a place in the city. People all looked like they had a spot; why didn't I feel like I did? I was a city boy, but I liked nature. I played football, but I didn't like violence. I liked girls but talked about how strange they were. It was plain to see I had too many disparities in my life. I couldn't find a spot where I had the answers, so I took a backseat to myself and let someone else drive the car. Who the other person was, I wasn't sure.

It may have been God. I was a believer. I had considered myself a Christian since my conversion in third grade. Still, I didn't know God. If God was running my life, I wasn't tuned in to it.

I liked my music at night before I went to sleep. The melodies of the songs and the personalities of the singers gave me a concept of life to hang on to in the ever-changing city life. The music bestowed a security I hadn't felt since I played down by Diamond Lake as a kid. I craved music. It was rock and roll, and it made me euphoric. The music would stay with me when I walked to school and back.

In fact, my friends and I discussed it a lot. We all knew the Beatles, the Rolling Stones, the Beach Boys, and the rest. It was a time when kids were grooving.

We were tuned in to music like birds into worms. Most of the songs were love songs, and we were still talking about germs girls would give us. However, we listened to the music while unconsciously fantasizing about love. I was interested in the way the musicians were trying to turn the world upside down. To me, it was funny. To my parents, it was scary.

The city held firm although divided between young and old, black and white.

The blacks all lived in poor neighborhoods toward downtown from our house or north of downtown. I didn't have any black friends, but a group of blacks was bused to my school from the inner city. I got to know a few of them from this experience. They listened to different music. I was curious about the blacks but did not find good opportunity to meet them. I wondered if we could get along. The one thing I noticed was that the few blacks I knew appreciated my kindness. They seemed to respect me for being a nice guy. It was as though it was unanticipated.

That day, the blue sky had no clouds at all. The panorama was great. I walked home from school on the warm fall day wishing every day could be so blue. It was the thing to do, to wish for more than we had. I could always have a bigger wish. The question was, could I live with what God gave me? I was a city boy. That gave me certain things in the immediate sense but also denied things. I had the chance to meet hundreds, maybe thousands, of people. However, I didn't have a lot of peace in my life, probably because so much was going on so constantly. I lived in a reputable community, but there were a lot of doubts and misgivings beneath the surface. It seemed like there was a counterpoint to every good point.

I would have gotten lost in confusion again if my parents hadn't pushed me along and if a decision hadn't been made by me to not try to figure it all out. I couldn't figure it out. Whenever I tried, I thought the adults were imbeciles and that I knew the way. I guess I felt like some of the musicians knew the way too. However, if I thought about it, the adults were confused. I could see so many of their foibles. They had the power, though, so I just didn't think about the situation. I just did my homework. Then at night, I smoked cigarettes with my friends. This seemed to get me by.

The next trip I took with my friends David and Tom was out to the suburb of Edina. David had to get an allergy shot at the doctor's office. We rode bikes on the freeway that was going up. It was called 35W and would soon service the whole Twin Cities. This night, we could ride our bikes on it, because it wasn't open to car traffic yet. It was so smooth that we really flew. As we left the city and got into the suburbs, I felt a kind of emptiness inside. The houses were all bigger and farther apart, which was interesting, but there were almost no people outside. It seemed boring. I was glad I was from the city.

That winter of my sixth-grade year in school, my cousins came to visit from California. It was my aunt and uncle and their two girls. It was a visit during Christmas so the girls could see snow. They all stayed at our house, and my brothers and I were set up to play with our two cousins. At first, they were nice, and things went well. However, shortly, they began to play up California and downplay Minneapolis. I for one wasn't going to let them get by with that.

"Minneapolis is the biggest city in Minnesota," I said.

"Yeah, but Minnesota isn't half as big as California," said my cousin.

"We're just as good as you," I came back. I felt like I wasn't going to let that sit.

"Minnesota gets all the fads from California," challenged my other cousin.

"What are you doing here, then?" I ended it.

I wasn't going to be labeled a hick or let Minneapolis be called a hick town. I saw Minneapolis as being just as good as anywhere else. I indeed loved my hometown, and I stood up for it. What could I say? My younger brother, Brett, was becoming a star athlete. My older brother, Fred, was a math whiz. I had to be something, so I was a loyal Twin Citian.

It wasn't just out of necessity that I loved my home city, though; there were some things particularly nice about it. It had size but not the problems that so often accompanied a city with size. I didn't see much crime. It was a fairly clean city in terms of appearance too. There were the lakes and the parks. Minneapolis was set out with lakes and parks like a picnic table is loaded with dishes at a church potluck. Harmon Killebrew, a Minnesota Twin, could have hit a baseball from my house to three parks and two lakes. I may be exaggerating, but my point is made. Besides the parks and lakes, we had a new freeway, a skyscraper in the Foshay Tower, and a world-famous theater in the Guthrie. I was happy to be alive and a boy in this great city. My parents gave me that feeling.

My relatives left to go back to California, but they also left an impression on me. Life was competitive. I saw how they pushed California. I saw the way I reacted and how I defended my city. Everyone didn't breathe Minneapolis. There were a lot of people who just didn't comprehend my relationship with my city. I knew it was special. I knew I had several dreams about the matter. I wanted to be a hockey star, not a piano player, and I wanted to become an important adult like a policeman or a teacher. I would always live in Minneapolis; there was just no other way. I was competitive about my home city. Still, I lived mostly inside myself.

The city influenced me through slow, methodical means into believing that it was all really happening. In the third grade, it had seemed like watching a movie. Now I felt like I was an actor in a play. It was all going somewhere. At night, the lights of the city made me feel it would never end. In a small town in the country, I knew there were times when it all died: went to sleep. In Minneapolis, someone was always awake. It made me a bit restless but more competitive than anything else. I wanted the city to be proud of me.

I wasn't sure how to go about it. The teachers had it one way, the musicians another. I could sense something out there that the city required in order to reward its mark of pride. Playing football was one way. It was competitive. It taught team values. Furthermore, it tested stamina and guts. I was a proud member of my home park's sixth-grade football team. Just playing football wasn't enough, though. I also did well in school. That helped my status in the city. I liked school, and my teacher was making sure that I worked up to my ability and also made sure I behaved. Doing well in school, however, also wasn't enough to win the badge of pride. I went to church. That was important. Not only did I go but I also believed. Still, that wasn't enough for me to really feel like I had earned sufficient merit in the city. I knew there was more. Maybe I had to be older. Maybe I had to get knocked around.

I found out my friend Tom People could be a bit of a bully. Not only did I get bumped in football practice by him, occasionally he would also just out-and-out bully me. We could be walking to school, home from school, or even be at school, and he would push me around. Sometimes it seemed like even the teachers would have a hand in it. I remember when I introduced him to Mrs. Never once. The first thing she asked was which of us was stronger, me or him. I had to do some hemming and hawing, because I knew he was stronger, but I didn't want to lose face. Still, Mrs. Never wanted an answer. I just said, "We have never fought." Tom just smiled. Mrs. Never smiled too. She had tried to pin me down, but I felt she hadn't. Tom probably bullied me as soon as we left the room; I can't remember for sure.

I thought to myself, *Getting knocked around—that's how to get approval from the city.* Maybe that's why I had become a rebel of sorts. Rebels got bounced around but still got respect. Jesus was a rebel.

Meanwhile, the city kept moving. There were new buildings going up, mayoral races, and professional sports. My body raced with the tempo like a cellist playing to a conductor, but my mind said, *Whoa*, like an economist says to inflation. My mind would have won out if it were my choice. If my mind ruled I would have stayed inside as much as I could, but my body needed activity.

Outside was crazy. However, my parents, especially my mother, deplored indoor escape as an answer to the city pressures.

I hooked up with Tom and Dave regularly, smoking cigarettes, getting bullied sometimes, and going to school every day. I was going to keep having a problem with Tom unless I figured out what to do. I couldn't complain to the adults, because that wouldn't be cool. I began to figure out that if I made Tom feel guilty, he wouldn't do it anymore. David also came to my rescue once when Tom was bullying me. Together, we convinced Tom to quit. I almost cried, in fact. That was the last time he bullied me. He always exercised self-control after that. I knew that deep down he cared about me.

When a person had friends, the city seemed like a good place. It all took shape for me without my knowing anything different. When I smiled at someone, they smiled back just as though we had a lifelong friendship.

This happened everywhere—on the bus, downtown, or at a sports game. People loved kids; I was at a good age for that. However, I still wanted to grow older. I wanted more experience, more exploration, and more friends. The school year ended.

In the fall, I started Ramsey Junior High School like a carrot sprouting out of the dirt seeking growth and sunshine. I quickly found it to be like a mixture of my fifth-grade and sixth-grade experiences. There were some kids who simply could not be controlled like in fifth grade, but the teachers strongly controlled those who wanted an education. I fell in between. I wanted to learn, but I also felt a strange compulsion to compete for attention with the class cutups. I was becoming an adult, but like the musicians I listened to, I wasn't a conformist. I was a mixture of salt and butter. The salt-iness came in my ability to stick with what I was being taught educationally. The butter in me was my total lack of control over a wide range of impulses. I maybe wasn't the worst kid in the class, but I did get on the teachers' lists rather early that fall.

I don't know what was wrong with me for sure. It may have been the need for attention, it may have been the devil, or maybe it was the competition to get to know the girls. I was shy face-to-face with a girl, but I could get some response from them if I became the funny boy in class.

Junior high was the first time I ever made wise-cracks verbally in class in front of the teacher, in front of everyone. I discovered license to express all the mischief in my soul. I didn't mean particular harm; I guess I just didn't think. I blurted out whatever came into my mind. I maybe had a way of making the students laugh; I thought they were laughing with me. Later in life, I would ponder this at great length. There were some people who I found would never laugh at me personally, and that was my family. They knew I didn't want to be laughed at, at least not in a way that made them superior and me inferior. In my family, we built each other up. Even though we teased each other and sometimes physically fought, we ultimately loved each other. My parents, especially my dad, saw to that.

And that's what the city was doing for me. I was only in seventh grade, but I felt I was beginning to master the city already. I could take a bus anywhere. I even had been over to the state fair in Saint Paul. I walked home from school on my own too. My perception of the city was growing somewhat. I was learning about the neighborhood away from home. I was also meeting people from different walks of life. I was confronted with new situations daily. I didn't know how, but I was determined to make it.

My mastery of the city was admittedly partial. It was just my boyish ego that fed any other dream. In most ways, I felt the city was unconquerable for me. I actually didn't even want to conquer it at all, to be honest; I wanted to make it my friend. I wanted to explore it.

I never thought the city as a whole would laugh at me. Most of the people didn't even know me. I didn't understand life that way. Individuals laughed—not communities. I wouldn't get laughed at too much, anyway. I was in with the cool kids. To laugh at us meant to laugh at something most of the kids respected. It would be like laughing at yourself. I made a lot of jokes, but I never thought I'd be the brunt of the joke. If it started in that direction, I always had the city to turn to or my family.

Perhaps I was turning toward God. I couldn't really understand it all. I had friends, and we were city boys. We respected each other, and there was no joke between us. Our private insecurities melted into defiance against anything that was threatening to us. We had all the answers, and if there was a situation where we were stumped, we put it off on others. We shrugged while drinking in acceptance somehow from the city at large. When we were wrong, we could always find someone in the city doing the same or worse. In that way, without us knowing it, God protected our freedom by allowing us to let others in the city be our escape mechanisms. We could always blame the adults.

The city was making more and more sense to me. I could focus on smaller phenomena like a bus ride or noticing a house I hadn't seen before, and I would make generalizations about the whole city. I would perplex my friends with generalizations like "Minneapolis is getting more sophisticated," when one black family moved into a white neighborhood. It was my nature to make broad statements about the city from only limited inspection of the facts. I guess I did that to understand life in the city. I knew behind it all there was consistency, so I tried to follow it and build my model in my mind of how things were. I was an amateur philosopher. Sometimes I bored my friends, other times they listened, and other times we argued. They had their own ideas about how things were.

In becoming a seventh grader, I at once had inherited a higher rank in the city and a shift to the bottom of the totem pole in the school itself. I was excited and let down all at once. Junior high was great, but seventh graders were the babes in the woods. If I hadn't had my friends to talk to, I would have been lost. It wouldn't be long. When I became an eighth grader, I would once again have status, and by ninth grade, I would be in the driver's seat. Seventh grade was like jump rope or hopscotch; everything was up and down. The upperclassmen were hard on seventh graders. The seventh graders themselves were still figuring out what was happening to them. The teachers were just trying to figure out how to keep the kids in their seats.

6

MOST OF THE time, I was drinking in what the city had to offer—that is, the movement or action of the people and the culture. I learned to see patterns in the city. People followed along similar lines. For the most part, people were law abiding and reasonable. As children, we watched the city people and lived out a reaction to all we saw.

I remained a nonconformist mostly because it seemed to be who I was. I saw myself as a servant-type person responding to the needs of others. I participated in life as one who was cast in a role. There were things I couldn't get out of life maybe because I was still a boy. I could see my adult life coming on for me, but it seemed so long away. There was so much I had to do. I especially wondered if I was ever going to get over my thing for nylons—or if I even wanted to.

My friends were starting to think I was smart, because I did well in school. If they were going to have this impression, I was going to have to work hard to keep up the image. I didn't feel like I knew that much, actually. There was a lot about the people I met in the city that I didn't understand. Everything seemed just out of my sphere of comprehension. My goal, though, was to understand it all. I was inquisitive. I always wanted the answer.

This was the '60s, after all. Every kid had a lot of questions. I was open minded enough to get some answers, but generally, that only brought more questions up in my mind. I questioned a lot, but I didn't question the power of the city. For me, that was a given.

The city meant to me a place to live, and it organized a style of life as a city boy I would live. I would see some things that would stop me cold, but there were always lessons to be learned. The city worked for the good of things. One had to see the bright side, or it didn't make sense. Even if something outwardly tragic happened, one could find an element of good and enough hope to go on. The death of Kennedy, for example, had been a loss, but on the other hand, determination to overcome became greater after the assassination. Likewise, a hard day in the city would only make other days easier in the city. There was discernible optimism.

I don't mean that life was easy, however. No, it could be very hard. Life in the city was unpredictable, not always just, and often stuffy. Behind the hard, though, was the soft, and behind the cold was the warmth. One just had to know where to look.

There were the girls. The city couldn't offer anything else as soft and warm as girls. We city boys were lucky. Yet it would take a long time before we could know how soft and warm they were. We didn't date or anything; we were just getting to know them.

I'll never forget the first time Tom and I went to a girl's house to pay a visit on a Saturday afternoon. I thought I was experiencing the greatest moment of my life. Sheila, the girl, was truly an inspiration to this young city boy who was in puberty. Walking home, Tom laughed at my excitement, thinking it was childish. I was a boy yet, so I didn't know what he expected. I knew city girls were the best thing city boys could find. I wasn't going to get mushy with girls, but at the same time, I could hardly wait to get older and taste the delight of female companionship.

For the present, I had to learn more about the city. It wasn't a studious approach; it was more like jumping with open eyes off a bridge into the lake. The only difference is that when you jumped open-eyed into the city, you never hit the surface. The endeavor became bigger and bigger and bigger with no point of getting off or down or out. The prospect of learning about the city became a one-way ticket into an unending trip. I was caught up in the merry-go-round.

The thing is, I thought I was in control. I felt I knew the truth. I didn't really try to put two and two together, but I felt the city functioned around my little circle. I thought that if I really put my foot down, I could always have my way. The musicians were singing just the songs I wanted to hear. There was rapport between us like magical connections that were stronger than anything else the city could offer. City kids had power. The momentum was going for us while the adults fiddled about nit-picking or worrying needlessly. They just couldn't reach me. Nobody could. I had been lost since third grade. The city defined what I was now. I was a seventh grader in junior high, I was a churchgoer, and I was trying to play park board hockey, which was my way of living out the dream I had as a city boy. Remember, I wanted to be a hero. I had to feel out the rules for this and also give considerably of myself. The city gave some, but it also took.

Some kids were just plain mean. I ran into the hard-nosed type as I never had before in junior high. They would steal your money, steal your food at lunch, or steal your clothes, and then maybe spit on you. They had no love of others. I learned for the most part to ignore them. They wouldn't come to anything.

On the other hand, I couldn't get over them. That type was an enigma to me. I wanted to be liked by everybody. Some of the meaner types certainly wouldn't like you if they could walk all over you. I had a dilemma. How was I going to get respect from kids who didn't care about me? I was going to have to stand up to them.

I remember a time when one of the bigger ones turned in the hallway between classes and punched me in the chest. Instead of cowering, I shouted, "What did you do that for? I didn't do anything to you. Why don't you pick on someone as big as you?" I dumbfounded him. He didn't think I would react that way. It was a tough situation until another guy came along who knew us both. He said, "Leave John alone; he's a good man." I looked at the bully and tried to make him understand that I really didn't want trouble. The pressure of the situation got to him, and he just walked away. That was the last time he bothered me. If I didn't have his respect, at least I got peace between us. What I was doing that bothered him, I just don't know.

I took courage from such situations. When I thought I had been up against an unbridgeable gap, a solution came about. If I had allowed myself to be bullied, how could I face the others in school? It certainly would not be cool. That maybe wasn't my main concern. Sometimes it didn't mean a plug nickel to be cool. What would the girls think, though, if I let someone push me around? They might think I'm sissyish. City boys were not sissyish.

Fall passed. Winter came. I joined the local park's seventh-grade hockey team. If I was ever going to be a star, I was going to have to work my way up. There must have been a gap in my thinking, because I was not even a star on that team. I'd have to think things out, but I knew one thing: I liked hockey even if I wasn't a star. I enjoyed being with city boys my age who learned that sports were a good outlet for young hearts searching for direction.

Competition, to a point, was the best answer for a pack of boys that could be had. A competitive spirit would get many a city boy through a lot of situations. A city boy had to feel competitive in the city at large.

There were dangers and snares to fall into, and an individual had to watch out for himself. In seventh grade, there were already drugs and drinking. It could have been a problem for me, but I steered clear even though I was just on the fringes of it.

I knew that if I wanted to be cool, I would have to be confronted with that some time in the future. To be competitive, I needed to be cool. There was just a whole lot I was going to have to face because I chose to be cool. I thought my decision to be cool was not half-bad. After all, the city was a cool place. I felt I must be cool to live in it. The situation was not like the '50s when one person in a group was cool; this was the '60s, and a lot of people were cool. I may not have gone that direction on my own, but Tom People kind of helped me along that path.

Maybe I would have been better off trying to play it smart. If I had grown up in a country school, I probably would have been an egghead. In the city, I was grooving to another beat. It was a time to discover life and to have friends and to do your own thing. I was learning about doing my own thing. I liked nature, sports, and TV—that's when I had a choice. My parents restricted me a bit; I couldn't do everything I wanted. Just the same, I had my own will, and even if I didn't do my own thinking entirely, I had a notion of what it was all about.

As a seventh grader, I was on the road to adulthood. I was learning things that would form me for life. The city was equipped to give me a rounded perspective from which to grow. I was growing slowly. It was like climbing a rope to the ceiling of a gym; the beginning seemed hopeless, but things got exciting the closer to the end that I got.

I was always thinking about the end. Whether it was the end of the week or end of the school year, I focused on finishing. Everything was moving. I was growing in body and mind like a plant in the spring. I didn't have stability. I had a need to keep going. My parents helped if things got rough, but most of the time, I moved forward on my own. I was always in a state of becoming.

My goal was to become a good adult in the city. I was curious how I would turn out. That thought occupied a great deal of my thinking. I was developing into a well-rounded city boy. The city had taken hold of my life.

It seemed so long ago that I had sat in my grade school classes and oddly wondered what was going on. At that period of my life, I knew what was going on. I felt a surety in my being like a bowler must feel to bowl a strike. I could sense the life the city was offering, and I pursued it. It offered excitement, rhythm, and gaiety of spirit. I liked all those things.

They came at me in school, at home, and on walks between places. I could run into a good time just about anywhere. The city allowed the capability for a boy my age to experience a considerable range of activity. The activity was building me into a better person. School, church, the home—all these places were there to facilitate a good life for me and others.

That spring, my family and I went to New York City on vacation. For three years, we had taken trips in springtime to various places in the country. The purpose was to broaden our experiences. It so happened that our time in New York coincided with the assassination of Dr. Martin Luther King Jr. It was a sad time with much upheaval and distress. I could see how the blacks were sad over the loss of their great leader. My family and I attended memorial services in Central Park where grown-ups cried openly.

I didn't really understand racism or what was behind it. I didn't know anything about judging a person by his skin color. I did realize that a lot of people were dearly attached to Dr. King, and like Kennedy, it was a terrible loss. I had learned some things about death since Kennedy's assassination. I felt anxious. So much that had been wrapped up now unraveled like a yo-yo.

My experience in New York gave me a thought about my experience in Minneapolis. One great man held so much together. He held such dreams. My thought was that it would be beautiful if everyone, especially in Minneapolis, could live out their dream. Dreaming had saved my life when I was younger. I was just now beginning to live my dream.

For one thing, I was getting to the age where I was becoming interested in the opposite sex. This is one of

the most exciting things that can happen to a young ad-
olescent. Naturally, I was awkward and didn't get very
far, but it was still quite a sensation.

Another thing that was happening was that I was
gaining a lot of new acquaintances as well as friends.
By springtime of my seventh-grade year, I must have
known a hundred people fairly well. This was quite a
jump from grade school. My life was expanding at a
faster rate than I knew how to cope with it. However,
it was more like a dream than anything else. I had fun.
Still, I had a sense of reality. I had to keep moving and
at the same time stay consistent. There was no niche for
me to hang my hat on.

I did have a home and good parents who helped,
but there was a lot I was going to have to do myself. It
helped that I was in with the cool kids. We liked to have
our experiences and our laughter. Yet there was respect
among us. We tried difficult things, and we took risks.
We were athletes. We were cigarette smokers. We all
liked attention. The excitement together took off the
harsh edge of reality. Minneapolis was like nuts and
bolts; you had to put things together before you came
up with anything that was useful. In my case, school,
church, family, and friends worked to keep me moving,
dreaming, and hoping. I hoped things would work out.

Oftentimes, I got through just by being able to laugh. It was a release for me from the situation. The city could get out of control if you couldn't laugh at it all. My friends and I were known for humoring life. It all seemed a joke.

Cigarette smoking, for example, was like smiling at the laws. We knew it was wrong, but we did it anyway, and with vigor. I'll never forget the time we smoked a whole pack between four guys in a half hour. We didn't want to bring any home. After the fifth cigarette, I dizzily walked home and got sick on the stairs up to my bedroom. My brother Fred realized what happened and tried to scold me, but I was too sick to hear. The humor of the episode was gone for then, but the very next day, I was smoking again.

7

BY EIGHTH GRADE, things were becoming complex. I had just gotten back from what was to be my last summer at camp to find out that Tom People's dad had died of a heart attack. I heard it through others who told me he died after doing heavy labor in his backyard. When I saw Tom, I didn't know what to say, so I said nothing. I felt ashamed about my silence like I had killed his father myself. The reason for my silence was my inability to say what I wanted. Of course I wished to extend sympathy, but I had a large struggle of my own going on. I sensed Tom's struggle, and I felt like it would be better if I just kept silent about it. Instead, we went out and threw apples at cars. I would always remember the time I just couldn't find it in me to express my sympathy. One day, I would have to come up with an answer for that. It made me feel a little weird.

There was also my situation in the city. Minneapolis was like a merry-go-round; a city boy felt like he was on a ride at a fair most of the time. The comparison fit, because the environment was carnivalesque, and the scenery was always changing, and you couldn't get off without stumbling. Now that I had withheld sympathy from a friend, I had the strongest desire to jump off the merry-go-round and take a break from the city. I couldn't find a way to do it, though. It's just that there was no available escape route. I had thought about suicide, but I didn't think I would really do that. I mostly had that thought in the back of my mind, and I could always find a reason to live. Somehow I would regain composure and a willingness to face Tom and others who I might have wronged, and then I would be happy. I could sense a happy life ahead if I just could survive blunders I committed, and if I could stay on the merry-go-round without falling off, I would one day enjoy the ride. I put great faith in the future. What else did I have besides the future? As an eighth grader, I had no great glorious past. As far as the present, it was chaotic, ever changing, and ever growing, so I could never live in it with much satisfaction. I was too awkward and too shy to want to take a good examination of my life in the present. However, the future was something I could think of at great length.

One day, a nice guy like me would be appreciated. I would lose my childish ways and become a thoughtful adult. I looked at the cool kids in class—I mean the really cool ones who were even cooler than Tom People. These kids were trying to be everything they were by eighth grade. They weren't going to have anything left by adulthood. I liked to think I was saving myself for a more important mission than eighth grade. Yes, the future and thinking about it is what kept me going in a lot of ways.

I still had my dreams. They kept me going too. The future held promise. I would resolve my life in the city by waiting until the proper time. I wanted to do the right thing. As an eighth grader, I was subject to a reality I didn't totally like. The adults had all the power and control. I realized that although I was still a kid, someday I'd be an adult and control my own life. I dreamed about being a hockey star in high school and becoming a college professor or something equally distinguished.

Life in the present did have some interest to me. I managed a lot of laughs with my friends like some of the times in gym class. It may sound crass, but we did rude things like urinate on each other in the showers. It was eighth-grade mentality. Another time, one of the so-called cool kids took a bowel movement in a urinal in the gym. Boy, were the teachers mad. He never got caught, though. It was the sick humor that had caught hold of my group of friends. It was actually too bad. Nonetheless, it was humor.

Then came the booze. I was introduced to alcohol at a gathering at one of the city boys' houses after school when his parents were gone. A bottle of bourbon came out of the liquor cabinet and made its way around the circle of boys. It burned in my mouth. I couldn't see how I was ever going to like that stuff, but I was surprised how quickly it became a habit later in life. At the time, it was an adventure for me, something new that brought me into the group and made me feel accepted.

I needed acceptance from the group. I guess I was proud to be in with the kids who were cool and who were doing things. I, too, liked the excitement. I didn't think about right or wrong. It seemed right, because in my heart I liked it. Why would it be wrong if I liked it so well? If it felt good, do it; that was the code of my generation. Were we wrong?

The only simple thing left in life seemed to be beautiful girls like Barbara Handsome. She had come a long way since grade school. I think she sensed her beauty and knew something about the power it held. She seemed to want to concentrate on improving her mind in school as if the beauty she had was a sidelight to the real self-worth she was trying to develop. I was watching her from afar hoping that someday I would be able to talk with someone like her in normal conversation. At the time, I kept my thoughts of her and other girls like her mostly to myself. I simply was strongly attracted to them but willing to let time run its course and letting the future hold my fate with such relationships. If it was right, someday a pretty girl would come my way. It was that simple.

Another thing that wasn't so simple was defining my relationship with the city of Minneapolis. It's not clear why I had to do that, but I wanted to. In times with my friends, we talked about Minneapolis. The consensus was that it was good. I felt that way. It could have been blind patriotism; still, I loved the city. I stood behind it. I took a rear seat to its up-front glory.

Minneapolis had a story like any other city. It was founded next to the Mississippi River, and it had an Indian name. It had a lot of lakes. There was a strong DFL (Democratic-Farmer-Labor) history, especially about Hubert Humphrey, who had been a mayor who threw the Mafia out and eventually became vice president of the United States. There were a lot of blond-haired, blue-eyed Scandinavians, but there was also a growing population of minorities, including a large population of Native Americans. The city was cosmopolitan but midwestern. It was a good place for a city boy to be.

A city boy I was. I wore GANT shirts and bell-bottomed pants. I had been downtown numerous times, and I had played touch football at many of the parks. I owned a three-speed bike and wore bumper tennis shoes or penny loafers for dress. I lived at a house with virtually no backyard with a basketball hoop facing the alley. My brother Fred was a basketball player. I wanted to be a high school hockey star, and I wanted a good job in the city when I was finished with school. If I had been a country boy, I would have probably been busy on a farm. If I were a suburban boy, I would have never experienced urban pride. I was a city boy wrapped up in the riches that come from being a little poor.

As expected, ninth grade came. It brought me another step along in my relationship to the Twin Cities. (I sometimes use *Twin Cities* interchangeably with *Minneapolis*.) I feel my life was affected by both cities, although mostly by Minneapolis. The two cities play off each other, and a resident of one is really led by both, but one many times claims the universality of his own city out of allegiance. By ninth grade, I had actually gotten all over the Twin Cities to sports games, concerts, restaurants, and parks. Things were cool for me. There wasn't a lot to say. I kept my mouth buckled unless it was to make a joke.

My generation was really doing battle with the adults. The city was the battleground. Whether it was music, hair length, or attitude, there was argument in the city. The black race was rising, the women were rising, and the youth were rising. Everything was getting hot. I sided with the rising faction. I felt like the city was with me.

It seemed natural to me that the city would welcome the freshness that my generation was putting forth. The adults had the power, but the kids were trying to be heard. Only God would decide who won and who would guide the city to its destiny. If I wasn't thinking about the conflict, I was trying to have fun. Marijuana was being introduced in our crowd. I thought it could be good. The idea of transcending trouble and getting high was enticing. I thought it could be a way out of the discord with adults and a door to appreciation of my environment from streetlights to pine trees to mansions by Lake Harriet. I looked to the crowd for fun; then I turned to the city for reward. Rewards were slow in coming and faint like the northern lights. I stayed caught between the security of my friends and the vastness of Minneapolis. Still, I found myself at the center of my life. I had continuity in my life. This city where I lived and was growing up in was like a steady beating heart that would always be there to give me sustenance and reason to live. I had wondered over it, competed against its forces, and adapted myself to its ways. I'd grown up a city boy, was still a city boy, and could not imagine what I would be other than a city boy. Everything beyond that was a dream or a hope. I had something now, though: I had an identity. My clothes, my language, and my feelings all conveyed the life of a city boy. I was firmly planted here.

I was fortunate to be rooted in my city. There was so much that could have gone wrong that didn't because of my ties to my home city. I kept busy doing things that strengthened the ties I had. I developed more friendships, played sports, and was going to confirmation class at church. That seemed to be a way to please my parents as well as develop a good attitude about things. I liked the city. I was attached to it in a way that caused me to follow a path laid out before me. The city offered life, and I accepted it.

School, church, my job as a paperboy, and many other things gave me a multidimensional existence. It may have seemed that things came my way via family or friends, but really it was God and the city that were fulfilling my needs. My family and friends fit in as actors and actresses in a motion picture that featured my life. The city was bigger than that. It meant give-and-take to me on a great scale. I had a relationship with an entity that was large and spread out. The city, about ten miles long and five miles wide, was the biggest affair in my life except for God. Maybe it was the way things came to me. I looked at the city to provide me resources. School, sports, and church were under the auspices of the city. I am not really saying that the city literally gave me these things; it wasn't quite like that or didn't seem that way to me. It was as if the city was there, and I was there in it, so the city took me on, and I took on the city to make it my home.

By *my home*, I meant that it was a shelter against the universe. The city had straight lines, square edges, and hard surfaces. Things were either parallel or perpendicular. It gave my young mind some walls to bump up against. Square buildings, straight roads, perpendicular intersections—I was always seeing structure.

In the country, I would have probably become an astronomer or something else concerned with a great, wide-open view of life. Maybe it would have been nice.

However, in the city, I was focusing on becoming a hockey player and perhaps a lawyer. My mind was tight. I thought about the practical, the economical, and the logical ways. Whenever I started to dream too much about the future, the city forced its way into my life with its demands, such as school and church. It was as though whenever I got too happy, the city was there to bump me. Then I had to grind my way through until I reached a point of relief.

The dark sky threw a chill through my football jersey as I biked after practice. I was a member of the Ramsey All-Stars, which was the ninth-grade team. We had Mr. Hacksaw as a coach, and I made quite a few friends on the team. That's why I played, really. I didn't like football, and I wasn't good at it. I had just parted from Tom People, having dropped him off at his house. It was nine o'clock, and it was the middle of October. Most of the leaves had changed and had fallen off the trees. The wind was blowing hard, and I thought to myself, *Someday, I'll be beyond all this. Someday, I'll be grown up, but sure as the sun, I'll look back and think of this as the good old days.* It was that thought that encouraged me to look for fun.

When Halloween came that year, I was too old to go trick-or-treating, so I went to a dance at my junior high school. I saw Barbara Handsome there, who by then was turning into a very pretty young woman. I got up the courage to ask her to dance, but she said no. I was discouraged, but I didn't think she was stuck-up or anything. I asked another girl to dance, who said yes. Dancing was no big deal. I had even kissed girls by then. I knew what intercourse was, but I hadn't gotten that far. Most girls seemed like they were saving something for a husband. That's how I felt about a girl like Barbara Handsome. She was not going to give away her love easily. Even in the Love Generation, love was not easy. I had felt rejection from Barbara, and it hurt. The next girl danced, though. Yet still I felt bad. Maybe it was the way I asked Barbara. Maybe she was just resting. Maybe she didn't like me.

8

IT WAS THE year hippiedom came to Minneapolis. It was a little shocking. Football season had just finished, and we had tied for city championship. My friends and I were all feeling good. Some of the team was made up of hard-core athletes. Others on the team were more susceptible to the hippie movement. I was one of those. Right after the season ended, I began to grow my hair out. My heretofore restrictive parents demurred to this new request that I be allowed to grow my hair down to my shoulders. The hard-hitting tackles of football were replaced by hugs and squeezes with girls at parties. Every Friday or Saturday night, someone from school had a party. Marijuana was a popular thing, and the music was psychedelic.

As a city boy, I grew on the relationships, the feelings, and the thoughts of my peers. It was a period when the kids were questioning everything. I remembered growing up with certain ideas about life in Minneapolis. I had thought I knew the difference between right and wrong. Now with the upheaval in society, things changed so fast, and it caused me to undergo deep thinking in order to survive. I had to reflect on many things. Were my parents all wrong? Was anarchy right? Were there any rules? I played it wide open with the feeling of a strong craving for experiences. The times were crazy with a lot going on that was new and different; it was a time for a city boy like me to aim for the sun.

The city was on fire. Children and parents tried to sort it all out, while businessmen tried to capitalize on the movement, and God commanded a strong presence in all that happened. Grace took a second seat to unbridled emotion. The minorities came alive with feelings and a desire for self-expression and status. Everyone had an opinion.

The city was being changed daily by the influences that came from the emphasis on personal freedom.

The music took a turn toward the political. Now the messages of the musicians carried newfound focus. It was spiritual. The artists were forming new fronts for people to gather toward. Music filled the city with a force that I found myself becoming very attracted to.

The music found me in my position as a city boy and gave me raison d'être. I was excited.

It was interesting to see all the changes around me. One never knew when he or she might see a car drive by that was painted up in some wild color or with political slogans or full of pot-smoking, long-haired youth. A young couple could be known to paint their house purple. Anything wild, anything far out—it was all happening in Minneapolis and Saint Paul.

Creativity was a large part of the newfound eccentricities. The urge to create was so strong and was inspired, by my theory, by the musicians and other artists. Everyone did their own thing. It was a nonjudgmental experience for me. Having the conflict I had with myself at a young age, coming out of it with a resolution to serve others, I was happy to facilitate anybody else's creative experience.

A lot of guys were using a line like that to get girls in bed, but I was truly trying to do the right thing. I wouldn't turn on anyone to marijuana who hadn't tried it before, and I didn't use women, either. I shared experiences with people who were already having them. I felt that if someone had chosen a path of experimentation, I would join them, because so had I.

The city was a great place to engage in shenanigans. For one thing, there were just a lot of people. You were always going to meet someone who was on some kind of journey. The possibilities were vast and uncharted. It seems like every weekend I was meeting new people who I smoked marijuana with, discussed politics, and learned something personal about. It was like a fever. I burned for more and more of what the city offered.

I remembered the derelict I had seen when I was downtown shopping. He wasn't the only one I'd seen, but he had made an impression. I am talking about the alcoholic I saw when I was with David Leaf and Tom People shopping for a football helmet. I had seen a type of beauty in him. I no longer thought of people like that as derelicts or even unfortunate. I thought they were closer to the truth.

I was concerned with the ultimate truths. I thought my friends were my truth, that girls were the truth, and that the city was the truth. Somewhere I remembered being taught that Jesus Christ was the truth, and somehow I still clung to that even though I kept that to myself. God resided deep within, and everything was hush-hush. I felt much freer to talk about simpler notions—or if not simpler, more concrete or touchable.

When winter came, the subject was hockey. That certainly was a more physical subject. I was at an age where play could get rough. I participated, but I was not really drawn to the violent aspect as much as to the grace of the sport. By ninth grade, a number of players were developing very worthy skills. They were worthy to be called stars. I wasn't of that caliber. A late bloomer, I felt that my best skating years were still ahead. I still hadn't given up the dream of being a high school hockey star, but I began to realize I couldn't bank on that too heavily, because it was clear to me there were a lot of players with better skills than mine. I was known to play "heads-up" hockey, and I was called a thinking player, but I never could have controlled the game on the ice the way some of the others did.

Still, I did not become deflated in my ego. I knew that I had some kind of calling. I knew that I would find another arena to verify my prowess. Every city has many children, and I felt that if I really tried, I would make my mark somewhere, somehow, just like the others. We would all make our mark. Every life in the city was sacred, and every person had a place. No one was left without love.

That's how I saw it even if the city did seem crazy to me sometimes. The adults were still confusing to me even though I was sure I understood what made them crazy. They were really preoccupied by their insecurities and weaknesses. They dwelled on failures and tragedies. Whereas the children were calling for a full-scale romp through life, the adults were sitting tight, mumbling about warnings of rude awakenings. The adults in control did not really know what to say about the youth who were arguing about everything.

I was finding a lot of fault with how things were. The Vietnam War was one focal point. I just couldn't understand why we were involved in a war half a world away that didn't concern us. Why should so many Americans have to die on foreign soil? To me, it was the big shots who were threatened and who were asking American youth to risk their lives.

As a city boy, I had witnessed all kinds of complexities involved in dealing with a lot of personalities in the city. We didn't resort to war in the city, however. I just couldn't accept why the world had to go to war, either. I wasn't alone. A lot of the city kids felt as I did. We were a peace-loving bunch in many ways. Our marijuana made us mellow while deeper values guided us.

I felt great being around a city where people were striving for higher principles. It was an experience of uniting my internal and external worlds. When I was young, I felt at odds with the city for the most part. I had felt estrangement and had suffered loneliness at heart-wrenching levels. The city had seemed alien to me. That was how I felt, say, in grade school.

Now in junior high with the movement of hippiedom and love, I really felt my need for a happy environment was coming into the realm of possibility. People were accepting each other and looking for the good in each other. At least this was true of some groups of people.

Other groups admittedly had conflicts. The youth and the adults were not getting along so well. However, even between them, dialogue was being established, and understanding was becoming more possible. We weren't always at each other's throats.

Still, blacks as a race were having a very hard time. There was a lot of talk about discrimination and racial prejudice. I knew and had made several friends with the blacks, many from football. I sympathized with their struggle for position and status in society.

Another group that represented over half the population was the women, and they were having very hard problems. Again, I sympathized. They made a good point in declaring that they were not being treated equally with men.

Despite all these disadvantages, people somehow kept the city going. It must have been hard work by people and/or the will of God. I'm not sure. What I did know is that I always thought things should get better. I was always, regardless of what I had, expecting more. It must have been the city that kept my eyes big—at least parts of the city did. It could have been my teachers, my minister, or my parents. It could have been all the constant action. Maybe it was the girls. Effortlessly, the gateway opened to more and more life. My situation was getting deeper and deeper, going right into the guts of the city.

It's lucky there was structure to guide me. I had school, church, friends, and family to help me with my direction. For the most part, all I had to do was jump through the hoops before me. I didn't even know what I was doing as I went along. I was virtually unconscious. That was the beauty of it.

The beauty in Minneapolis was also inspiring. There were the beautiful girls who I thought about all the time. There were the beautiful parks and lakes that were a true inspiration to all. In addition, there were the seasonal changes. We had a midwestern, four-season year. Fall started my school year, winter came and challenged our endurance, spring weakened us and took our breath away with its beauty, and summer set us free.

Considering everything going on in the '60s, I think I was most affected by the beautiful things in life that occurred and what people did.

Whenever we smoked marijuana, we would walk around for hours just trying to understand a tree or a streetlight. We were so self-absorbed. The mood of the group was so frivolous and spontaneous.

We were going to change the city. People like us were destined to do things. Bright horizons loomed before our eyes. Beauty and curiosity were calling us forth. We were idealists. Perhaps we saw the potential of the city, and we wanted it realized. Whatever we were, we had an affair with the city. It held our dreams and aspirations. As city boys, we were garbed in pride for our city. I guess that made us idealists.

9

MY IDEALISM GREW at multiple rates that summer between ninth and tenth grade when I attended a summer program put on for talented youth. It was an experience of sheer growth. Everything I held as true was put into question. I found out how little I really knew. The program ran somewhere between a philosophical enlightenment and a toe-smashing outlook on society. I got up every morning early to take the bus to school. My parents were surprised at my diligence, and so was I. The classes were designed to call a person my age into a higher calling. I was challenged to form values and think out my life. The classes gave me vision for how my life could go. There were possibilities to see a new way.

I had always thought I knew where my life was going. I was going to be a hockey star and then get an important job downtown. At this school, however, all these dreams I had were called into question. I now became interested in freedom and getting to know in a deeper, philosophic way. There were a lot of students who were freeing their souls and baring their feelings. It was a time of great change in my life.

I was called into a new philosophy of life. I was called to become responsible. This was foreign to me in some ways. I smoked cigarettes, caused problems for teachers, and acted up with my friends. Yet the summer school was teaching me higher values. It was instructing me to create ideals and live by them. The school was teaching me to love my fellow man and be sensitive to everyone.

The new calling felt good, and I thought I was ready. I would quit some of my erroneous behavior and shoulder some of the burden in life. It was time to grow up. The city was a place really where I could take advantage of its many offerings. I had always used its parks, lakes, schools, and churches, but now I could use them differently.

I could begin to communicate my feelings and ideas to others who were also city dwellers. We could begin to reflect on our city lives rather than run around aimlessly.

I still wanted a place in the city, but not for the same kind of reasons and not the same kind of place. Now I was a thinking city boy. What things I had endured before now became objects of contemplation.

Instead of blindly accepting city life, I called everything into question. The environment I had grown up in appeared now as incomplete or mixed up. I always knew there were problems in city life, but I never had much of a solution; I had just gone along with the flow or turned into a rebellious sort with no clear intentions of creating anything better. At this school, I was beginning to see a light in the direction of responsible activism. I truly wanted to sort out the rights and wrongs. I didn't like the fact I had worn my mother's nylons and I also had a problem with any bullying I had done. I couldn't accept wrongs quietly; it made no sense to me to even try. What I saw was that the city was screwed up. There were many things wrong.

Good souls were being lost like that old man with the bottle I had seen as a youth. He was just one; there were many like him. It was obvious; things were not going my way. I wanted to see the light in people's eyes increase, get brighter. Everywhere I looked, people seemed to be losing that spark. I had once seen a really lively element of the city in people's eyes. Now I could only see for the most part sadness or madness. Oh, perhaps I was just going through a period. I could forget it all for a while if I concentrated on having fun and keeping my sense of humor intact. I knew there was the bad in life. I was okay with that as long as the good outweighed it. Carefully, I chose how to proceed with my life in view of all that was confronting me. School, problems, relationships—all were cast in a way that I could either make the best or worst of.

Logically, I chose to make the best of my city life situation. A city boy knew how to survive. The summer school session went on, and I learned more and more about possibilities in life. I tried to tie all these ideas into my role as a city boy. I could see how humor, goodwill, and effort would play a role in my life. The teachers taught us to think big and also creatively. I was all for that. Even more, the teachers taught us to feel and to be tender and sensitive. I was really that way.

One might not think that a city boy would have such feelings. One might think the city would destroy such a thing. No, it didn't in me. I looked around and saw all the city people, and it stimulated me, invigorated me. My parents had always pushed me to get out and do things. At times, I hadn't felt like it, but that's when I was younger. Now as a ninth-grade graduate, I thought of myself as a sociable human being. If there was a day I wasn't doing something with others, it seemed empty.

At the school and in my neighborhood, I kept busy doing things. It was my way of adapting to the environment. The city moved, and so did I. The idea was to stay with the movement and maintain my existence. I had to be active.

I also had to remain cool. The city was not a place for hotheads; there was too great a chance to get hurt. Too many hotheads meant a fight. No, I chose to be cool. It was an image. It was a lifestyle. It was how I survived. Luckily, my friends were cool, and we were accepted as such, at least at school. Whether the city would ever see me as cool, well, that was something I was striving for. My childhood dream really was about acceptance. In the school, I was really trying for acceptance. What I really needed from the city was that kind of acceptance. I searched for that by being cool.

Such a thing was not easy to come by. There were a lot of things that could cause one to break down, to lose his or her cool. I maintained a steady focus to achieve what I felt being cool was about. It was loyalty to friends, it was composure, and it was being true to yourself.

When I started high school that fall, I knew things were going to be different from junior high. For one thing, my dad was a teacher at the same school I attended. That could either make or break me. I liked my dad.

In fact, I loved my dad. However, we were coming into a situation where we were going to have proximity in a social environment. How would that work? I decided to proceed with a low profile. My brother Fred had led the way. He'd been in the situation for two years. I would act like it was the most natural thing in the world to go to a school where your dad was a teacher. If school proved tough, what would I do? School had always been the safest place in the city for a city boy. If I couldn't get along in school, life was certainly going to be full of turmoil.

The first few days went great. My dad's path and my path did not cross. Well, several teachers made a big deal out of the teacher's kid bit, but I just smiled. It was clear to me that I would be under some kind of special scrutiny. I accepted it like being a city boy. I grew in the role. Maybe I would even like it.

It became important for me also to be nice. This may not sound like a lot for a city boy to be, but I had to be nice, really, if I wanted people to be nice to me. There were those in my life who would say I wasn't nice and, in fact, quite mean; however, this was a fault of mine not to be confused with my real desire to get along and be well liked. I wanted to be considered a nice guy.

Any meanness came from frustration. It could have just been city life. With so many people and so much going on, it was hard to be nice to everyone in an individual way. Like my experience in grade school, it was still difficult to always do or say the right thing. Things were so busy.

I did get the opportunity to talk with friends and have real heart-to-heart talks. We communicated at length on our true desires, our hopes, and our dreams. Much of the talk was about our relationship with the city.

"Do you think you'll stay in Minneapolis when you grow up?" asked Tom one day when we were walking home.

"I don't know where else I'd want to live," I said.

"I wouldn't like a small town at all," said Tom.

"No, me either."

"I always feel there's a lot to do here."

"Yeah, we've got all the parks and lakes."

"This is a heckuva city."

"Yeah." The conversations were simple but defined a certain attitude.

The red sun went down quickly in the west. I was just getting home from school. I was late because I had stayed after to watch the varsity football team play a game. I didn't play football anymore myself; I was waiting for the hockey season to begin. Football was too violent for me. Hockey could get rough, but it was also a game of finesse. I wasn't really big, so I thought a game of finesse was more on the right track for me. A city boy had to be careful about what he chose to do with his time. To me, sports were just a game. I couldn't take them that seriously. Schoolwork was much more important for my interests; I was a studious type. I enjoyed learning, and my parents were happier when I got good grades. A good education would open doors for me in the city.

Minneapolis was a raw and undefined place. It was almost chaotic. To follow my dreams at all, I would have to do well in school. It had always been that way ever since grade school. In consequence, I kept one eye on school and the other on the city. Putting both eyes together, I fashioned a dream about how my life would work out.

I was beginning to find limitations in myself that could stop dreams I had earlier in life. I was never going to be a hockey star. Realistically, I knew there were a lot of players with more ability than I had. However, my dream became more alive in the area of making something of my life. I did well in school, and I was ambitious. I didn't really know what the city was going to offer me or what I would attempt to do, but I did have high expectations. With so many people so close to-gether, something was bound to happen. Nothing did. The city just took on more and more personality, and my attitude toward it didn't change. I felt like I was at an advantage over many other people by living as I did in a city. My identity really came from the city. I was proud of the Twin Cities.

For me, this caused some cockiness and a kind of mental toughness. I might also have been aloof. I really couldn't claim to know everything, but I really thought I had the big questions answered. I had all the facts down and all the angles figured out. I could work the city. It was like a machine to me. It was a place to flourish—or at least it was a respectable place to hang my hat.

As far as my needs were concerned, the city did okay. With respect to a psychological analysis like Maslow's pyramid of the structure of human needs, the city satisfied at least my basest needs. I did not go hungry or thirsty. My security and protection needs were also met, especially by my parents and the police, but my higher needs, such as social, were only partly fulfilled, and highest needs like self-actualization and esteem were still to be found. I would have to wait for that.

I had something inside me that ticked like a clock. I was full of compulsions, questioning thoughts, and a rash of indecisiveness. On top of that, I came off as shy. Out in the country, I maybe would have been left alone or been molded by some small-town ideas into a small-town personality. In Minneapolis, it was between me and the city as to what kind of person I would be.

It could be anything. There were times and things that seemed to be wrong or out of sync with what I thought. I could have the experience of life going against me.

Consider my feelings toward Barbara Handsome. She hardly noticed me at school, yet I lived for her smile or kind words. Oftentimes, they never came. There was also the hunger for success exemplified by some of the students. It didn't mean much to me. I really thought I should be more important to my friends than any material gain.

That's what the hippie movement was all about to me. It was about love. I considered myself a hippie of sorts. I was an urban version of a free spirit. To me, the powers of the city were humorous, because I viewed it all from the position of an outsider. I was a city boy and not an admirer or supporter of the status quo. I wanted change.

I had to think something. I looked to the future. The present was a painful experience. Things were not my way. I was a rebel who chose to be against a lot of what went on. I was against all the hypocrisies and inconsistencies. I saw right through it all. There was a lot wrong that I just couldn't go along with. Why were some people poor while others had so much? Why did I have to learn things I didn't want to know? When would my time come?

I was somewhat self-righteous about the whole thing. Inside, I knew more awaited me, so I wasn't going to make a fool out of myself trying to grab everything in high school.

Besides, there were some different twists coming at me like the hitchhiking experience I had. I had hitchhiked many times without any real problems. It was a way that I showed my trust in people and my free spirit. However, I had a bad experience that left me cold. Three young men picked me up over by the school one day when I was hitchhiking. I was only going a short distance. Immediately, they began to badger me, and then they wanted my watch. When I refused, they said they were going to shoot me. We went back and forth at it; finally, I took off my ten-dollar Timex and handed it over. They let me out with no physical harm done. Psychologically, though, I'd been hurt. I had trusted them, and they had proven to be criminals. I was mad.

In the city, though, there wasn't time to be mad long. I was back in the swing of things in no time. I couldn't concentrate on others who did me wrong. The movement of the city carried on; I couldn't stop to try to think of how to make things better. Life was a given.

10

IT FELT LIKE the city was really eating up my personality. It took chunks out of me here and there as though it had the right. Take those criminals, for example. They were only acting upon conditions that made them that way. It was the city that did that to them.

In many ways, though, I liked the Twin Cities. I wouldn't move anywhere else for anything. However, I wished I could stop the senselessness of it all. Why couldn't people just say what they felt in their hearts? There were so many games people played and games I played.

I thought I was becoming real when I went to that summer school. Things seemed to matter, and the students were honest and straightforward. I was convinced that I was on the road to adulthood and into my dream of finding a niche in the city.

Then came high school. Peer pressure was greater than ever. I discovered the high school kegger. People would buy several kegs of beer, and we would drink until we were in a stupor. I remember my hesitation to participate in this kind of thing. It seemed to be right out of status quo. I wasn't sure I wanted that scene in my life. However, my friends all went, and so did I.

Because of it, I was having an experience of becoming acquainted with new neighborhoods and particularly the homes of many people. The attraction was the keggers, but as a benefit on the side, I got invited to many houses where the parties were being held. City homes were actually where life took place. Oh, schools had their place, and churches were important, but the major driving force behind the city was the houses and the families that lived in them.

Being in someone's house was like being told a secret about that person's life. I still kept track of my schoolmates and was devoted to remembering them separately or jointly, because I cared about them and had an interest in all of them. When I got invited to their parents' homes, it was like filling in information that had been missing. It was very vital for me to have that kind of experience.

It also felt like my life in the city was growing as I intended by going to parties in all these houses. It was truly an experience. I could witness how all these associates of mine actually lived. It was a real growth experience to see the variety and to sample all of it—that is, the city as broken down into homes.

I found refuge in homes like the country boy finds in farm fields. People's homes were where I checked in to maintain relationships with friends and get perspective on differences of lifestyles among the people of the Twin Cities. My friends' homes told a lot about them.

There were my richer friends who lived over by Lake Harriet. Jack Johnson, a person I had met in junior high but with whom I became better friends in high school, lived in a huge home over by the lake toward Minnehaha Parkway. We often went by his house to get him when we would go out on a Saturday night. Eddie Fastone had his license, and we sped around South Minneapolis until midnight when we had to be home.

My point about the houses, though, was concern with the keggers we had in them. At Jack's house, when his parents went up to the cabin for the weekend, Jack had us all over for a party.

There were a lot of folks I knew—Newt Full, Eric Rock, Tom People, Dan Ran, Scott Flight, Debbie Gate, Linda Baby, Colleen Champion, John Followup, Barry Ash, Buzzy Nor, Randy John, Tammy Lee,

Sarah Steve, Beth Hut, and Barbara Handsome, plus many others.

Jack had a nice house. We never trashed it too badly. We tried not to be too rough on the furniture, and we even took off our shoes at the front door when we came in. We had that same respect for each other that I had had with Jim Hoknoski as a grade schooler.

City boys had to respect each other, or they could end up fighting or worse. We could joke with each other, but we valued each other's person and property.

I knew Jack's house was bigger than mine; however, in the end, they were both homes and served as such. The only observation I made was to see how it was kept up and decorated. I didn't say anything to Jack; I just knew what I liked and what I didn't.

At times, at these keggers, I felt the city was at bay. I was protected by the shelter of the homes, safe in my alcoholic stupor.

The parents of my friend Jack or any of the parents of other friends whose homes were used for keggers were the people who really seemed to own the city. If I was within one of their homes, what ill could befall me? I wasn't overly fearful or vulnerable. Mostly, I was interested in having some laughs and being with my friends, whether it was big homes like Jack's or smaller homes toward the inner city where people were poorer.

We could sit around the kitchen table or in a living room and crack silly jokes for hours.

Barry Ash asked, "Did you hear about the poor barber's years-old comb?"

Jack Johnson replied, "No."

Barry finished, "He couldn't part with it."

I asked, "What do you get when you mix a computer with a gorilla?"

John Followup said, "I don't know."

I replied, "A Harry Reasoner." The stupider the jokes, the more fun we had.

Sometimes, we would talk about school stuff, the football team, or teachers we didn't like. Other times, we would talk endlessly about the flavor of the beer. The girls would always remind us how dumb we were.

11

IF I HAD focused my city experience on houses in the tenth grade, then eleventh grade was concentrated on my close friendship with four of my schoolmates. There were Jack Johnson, John Followup, Dave Surf, and Barry Ash. Whatever thoughts I had had about what Minneapolis was were changing. I now realized it was a zoo, and we were the animals. The five of us were wild almost beyond any level of responsibility. We smoked marijuana, drank beer, and drove drunk around the city between the times we were wantonly vandalizing property.

It's not that we didn't have consciences; it was more that hormones powered us to unsafe levels. We were not going around hurting people, but we did break their laws and damage property. To this day, I don't know what caused us to think this was okay—part of it for me was still my rebellion against the status quo. I was upset by the inequalities and injustices of the city. For another thing, I still hadn't worked out my thing for nylons.

I felt miles apart from girls who seemed to guard their bodies like gold.

I developed feelings for the political events in life. Take the black struggle, for example. I was sympathetic in a lot of ways to what the civil rights movement was all about. How could blacks end up with so little? To me, it was a wrong that glared in the face of humanity.

That was just one area of injustice, though. I was upset about things in general. I wasn't at the point, though, of dropping out of society to be a total hippie; I just played out my anger through wanton acts of vandalism. The girls that knew us in school had no idea that we were doing these kinds of things at nights and on the weekends. One reason school was probably as calm as it was had to do with the presence of the feminine element. There was only one thing stronger than the male hormone, and that was the feminine sense of decency. It kept a lot of young men in line who were trying to please them.

We acted the roughest when we were away from girls. We would often erupt into fights among ourselves that would even get violent. It was in the spirit of fun, but it was out of control. The city seemed to accept this violence as boys being boys. I can remember the police seeing us several times and catching us at something illegal and dismissing it all with a stern word and no arrest. I respected the police. I knew they had the authority over me to take my freedom away. I tried my best to stay on their good side. Either police or girls kept us in line.

I was really trying to do the right thing. I wanted to stay on the good side of everyone. I was concerned about my popularity and image. It was cool to cause trouble, but one didn't want to cause trouble to the extent of getting in serious trouble. This was especially true if one's dad was a teacher at the high school one attended.

My family meant a lot to me. My dad and I were in close contact, my mother and I were on good terms, and I got along fine with my three brothers. Fred had gone off to college with his good mind and had become politically active, Brett was developing into quite an athlete, and Keith was coming along in grade school.

I was left in high school with a city-boy yearning for experiences, good humor, and a good reputation. I wouldn't do anything to damage any of that. The city didn't ask much of me at this time, just that I go to school and be a good citizen. I'm not sure how I measured up—probably not to full standard. I attended school all right and even did well, but the animals I was friends with were not leading totally upright lives. We weren't really bad, but we were not everything society or God expected of us.

I hadn't been in a church since confirmation. I had become bored and alienated from it. I turned to God in moments of solitude, though. I still had my moments where city life overwhelmed me and when I would have to take refuge in the tranquility of spiritual things. I was always surprised that God loved me despite some of my errant ways. I turned to God regularly in what could loosely be called prayer and at moments I just didn't want to go on. I even thought of suicide as a solution to get out of the crazy patterns of city life. I had to really struggle sometimes to find good reasons to go on.

These moments, however, were usually short lived, and the city threw a good omen to me to call me back into the right way of thinking. Oftentimes, it was a girl. I would take a fancy to some cute high school student, and I would be preoccupied with that for weeks. There was also schoolwork, which in general I was interested in. I liked learning and was good at it. It was only the times I looked at the city as a whole that I got discouraged.

If I took it down to its basic components—for example, houses—I could enjoy my experience. When I thought about the great scope of the city, like all the houses, people, and buildings together, I was almost floored. It was too much, simply too much.

Luckily, as had always been the case in my life, I had friends to turn to. I had a conversation with a girl, Colleen Champion, who showed me a great deal of understanding. We somehow got into a conversation about suicide. I had told her that I had thought of it. It had become the only way I thought I could escape the city hypocrisies and general falsehoods.

She said, "Don't do it. There are a lot of people who like you. You would hurt a lot of people who like you. You would really hurt a lot of people. You're not considering it for that reason, are you?"

"No," I said. "It's just that I think the city's a crazy place."

"The city could make sense to you someday. You could get right with things," she said.

It was the greatest hope that had been offered me in a long time. It was that good omen that I'd been looking for. I felt relief. Yet things weren't going to change overnight. It seemed that expectation of reason in my city life only cast deeper shadows on the confused reality I faced.

Instead of retreating, I approached life with a renewed rebellion and a new carelessness. I drank beer at keggers as if I didn't care a hoot anymore. It was becoming almost funny; the whole situation could almost have gone up in laughter. Still, it was not totally a joke. I retained some hope that Colleen was right.

Plus I liked school, and I did have some concern about life and others. I also believed in God. God in my life had become relegated to a spirit I turned to in hardship. I felt no joy in God in the good times. God was only a comfort for me to seek when all else failed. I am not sure why there was this distance between God and me; perhaps it was because I was doing so many things wrong. Was I still trying?

12

MY SENIOR YEAR would really have a strong effect on my life. I would receive honor and challenge. In the fall, I was chosen as homecoming royalty. I should go into this a bit. When I found out about it, I outwardly scoffed and acted as though I didn't want to be a part of something so status quo. Inside, though, there was undeniably a part of me that was honored as if I were special or even good looking. I went through the ceremony with one hand pushing it all away and the other hand extended and grasping all the attention, all the applause. I felt a little phony. Was I becoming somebody I didn't like? There were these questions. Again, I didn't have time to get answers, because in the city, every day brought new concerns. Homecoming dilemmas were left hanging. It had been a thrill, though, an addition to my life and way of thinking. I had become a thrill seeker.

Once again came the high school keggers. As seniors, however, they seemed to have more class for us. Oh, I admit, I still got sick at most of them, but up to that point in the evening, the twelfth graders were on top. The athletes really ran the things. I wasn't an athlete; I had dropped out of hockey to concentrate on my studies. Yet I was on friendly terms with them. The football team actually had a lot to be proud of; they had won the state tournament that year and hadn't lost a single game the whole three years I had gone to the school. The girls were ecstatic about it. You could always talk about the football team with them at the keggers.

Meanwhile, I kept thinking about my role in the city—now and the future.

I was shy by some standards, but I was funny. Maybe I could become a comedian with the candid understatement. I would bust up everybody by combining the everyday with the absurd, like:

"Did you hear that Mayor Stenvig is resigning?"

"No."

"Yes. He's decided to be the leader of gay rights." The idea of Stenvig, a law-and-order mayor, leading a gay rights cause was absurd. It was the kind of thing I could say and it would be funny, at least at keggers.

I wasn't sure where I was going in the city. I knew I wanted to live there, I knew I would soon be on my own, and I knew things were getting closer to a time for decision. I liked booze, I liked the company of women, and I didn't have a clue how to make a living or what I desired to do. I was a city boy; that's it. That's the way it was. None of us knew what we wanted to do.

As twelfth graders, we were really on the edge. We wanted to celebrate the culmination of our public education, yet we knew we faced the city without school as a barrier to its harshness. How would we fare? What directions would we all go? We were building up the tempo with no idea where we would be let off.

My four animal friends, as I thought of them, and I were actually going to be split up. We were going separate directions to college, to work, to wherever. It would be different. Whatever else could be said, it would be different. I'm sure all the others in twelfth grade felt this too.

I received other honors, including being selected to be in the National Honor Society; being in Millwheels, the school talent show; and representing Washburn High School at Boys' State, a VFW-sponsored weeklong program that taught local government skills. These honors made me think I was well on the road to my dream of becoming a star in the city—an adult with power.

When it came time for senior graduation, we had a party. It was the last hurrah. We partied with a vengeance.

The night had begun with graduation ceremonies. We showed ourselves to be in the mood for partying when, against all rules, we threw our graduation caps into the air at the ceremony's conclusion. The teachers went wild, but what could they do? We were going to be out of their hair now. Before the party began, I went home to my parents and met with them and my grandparents, who charitably wished me good luck. I drank a little punch, and then I was off to meet my friends.

Jack, John, Dave, Eric, and I drove down by Minnehaha Creek where we got loaded on beer and marijuana and hashish in order to get primed for the party that night. We were totally excited and full of piss and vinegar.

We sauntered over to Washburn High School, where we'd attended, and got on the bus that would take us around the city to three different locations. It would be our all-night, farewell graduation party. We were shouting and clapping, and there seemed to be nothing that could stop us. The city would never stop me now.

13

I THOUGHT THE city would never stop me, but in the fall after graduation, I left for a small town in southwestern Minnesota to go away to school. I had left the city for a place in the country.

At first, I spent my idle time getting into nature. I took long walks through the arboretum by myself, smoking marijuana to peak my experiences. As far as drugs went, I also began drinking beer like a wrestling fan. I was trying to bring synthetic highs into my being, possibly to escape the boredom I felt for country life. I felt isolated. I looked back on my city life that I had as a young boy, and I thought that was when I really had freedom when I could do things with a variety of people. I was losing the momentum of the city.

For the most part, I liked the education I was getting, but I really needed to get back to the city. Maybe then, everything would be okay. Life was getting pretty wearisome in that small town. Except for losing my virginity, it was uninspiring.

I transferred my status to the University of Minnesota back in Minneapolis after two years in the small town. It needed to be that way. I took a year off from school before starting at the U of M and spent time traveling in Europe with my college friend Rick. In Europe, we spent most of our time in cities, naturally. When I did get back to school in Minneapolis, things seemed better for me.

I spent two years at the university to get my degree—time that went by quickly. What I really noticed was two things: I liked school in the city better, and I was doing a lot more drinking.

Then one night, I had an experience that would change my life totally.

I was driving in downtown Minneapolis at breakneck speeds, dead drunk—on a night when I found out that a former girlfriend was now sleeping with a friend—and I had a terrible car accident. I ran into a stoplight, and I cracked the windshield of my car with my forehead while racing with that new boyfriend of my ex-girlfriend.

I was never the same after that. My thinking became much more desperate. In quick succession, I had a religious experience that would even more fully change my life. I sensed the presence of an angel, which gave me relief and direction in contrast to my psychological distress. The conflict in me grew, and I began taking psilocybin mushrooms to get a high. It wasn't all bad. In the city, one was faced with many angles of life, and one had to live out his own life as best he could even in unforeseeable events like car accidents, broken relationships, and angels.

That's how I had thought of the city. It was a place . . . a geographical location . . . a place on earth where people lived . . . a place that was stagnant and permanent. The hit on the head, the drugs, the break-up, and even the religious experience led me toward a crisis in my life—psychosis. I would have a new understanding of what a city boy was now. My mind was recreating all the boundaries it once had made.

The city was really people. I realized that as I stepped out of a mental ward in a hospital where I had spent the last two weeks as a patient. I stood under the bright sun looking at the leaf-filled trees and watching people walk by. I felt alone, but I sensed myself as one of many persons in a kind of play that featured us as actors and actresses of the city. It should have been obvious to me before, but now I really understood that there was no city without people.

I felt a certain lack of resolve, but now my lack of resolve was so poignant that I became resolved in a different way. I took my experience as a spiritual one; I was a born-again Christian. I was very uncomfortable, but years of drinking and drugs had turned me into a psychologically experienced person. I could handle mental change.

The city went on. People with business suits strode down the sidewalk looking like they already had experienced this feeling of upheaval. They didn't seem to be connected to the sidewalk they walked on; they were connected to other people. Mothers walked by with their children and were holding their hands tightly as if they knew these unspoken truths of the city—that the city was a mishmash of people. It wasn't buildings or land.

The city would be a new experience for me now, but I would still be called to do the right thing. Now that I had come to realize the city was made up of people who defined what the city was, I took a much different attitude, and things were in a new perspective. The garbage in the streets smelled; the airplanes overhead were loud; the grass in the park needed mowing. I felt and sensed everything about the city now, because it all seemed to be a new awareness for me. I could barely think about being some kind of star in this situation;

I was just surviving. It seemed like I hardly knew what the city was.

That was ghastly and unnerving, but there was challenge. Others were challenged to stay alive amid this chaos that they already understood. I was challenged to go forth with a new view of the city. I had to sort this all out. The chaos had to make sense to me in terms and laws and codes of love. That was my challenge.

The love people had in their lives was what the city was about. Love gave people the courage to walk down the street. The city ran on love. Love was the glimmer in the eyes of city people.

However, there seemed to be a great distance between people's heads and hearts. I could see great pain in these strangers' lives; yet a lot of them had a smile on their faces. The whole situation seemed upside down. People seemed to grip at heartaches like young lovers gripping at bodies, not realizing their focus was incomplete. Only a small tip of their lives seemed to be truly content. Yes, some were smiling, but their feet were moving like stumps of wood—like they had no feeling in them at all. Others seemed too eager about life in the city, and others only held a distant glaze.

Some of the people appeared to have some concept of love, but they were not living the love that was inside them. The city had little or no soul. The place that had once been a tangible domicile was for me now a shaky conglomeration of strangers on a path they could not see. Their lives and their hopes were miles apart. The city did not make sense like it once had. I was seeing it from street level where the city really existed.

I walked down the sidewalk smiling at the people as they walked by. This is what the city really was. It was people. Almost four hundred thousand people is what Minneapolis was, four hundred thousand people who all thought differently and looked different. The nice package I had built as a youth did not hold anything now.

There seemed to be such confusion and much effort aimed at ending the confusion. I could see that the people had an attitude, but it seemed that they were drowning in their own sadness. At the same time, there was an air of desperation and a slight unwillingness to lend anybody else a hand. It almost seemed inhuman if I were to pass judgment.

The city as a whole could not be grasped mentally at any one moment. It was too big, too unruly. As I walked down the sidewalk, I realized that the city where I had once been a warm observer now enveloped me and sealed me as an active participant. I became part of the city, and the city punctured my being.

Maybe if I had been in the country, I would not have felt so transparent, so uptight. Here I was in the city, however, and life was uneven and stressful.

What I had been able to grasp and have a handle on now was a disjunct, sketchy blur. There was no method to it. Everyone seemed in such a hurry, and it didn't look like they were really going anywhere.

The city was a place where people lived, a place for people by people. People came first. They defined the city. And I noticed that the people were hungry. Spiritually, they were starving, and they were cold emotionally. They were not really outwardly mean, but they showed the chill of their being in their eyes. The people looked but did not look. It was kind of awkward.

The city had nostrils and legs and arms. It encouraged effort by one but left one in immediate nowhere. There was no answer for someone. One traveled on faith or some other vehicle. The city was upside down. I had trouble breathing. I didn't know how to take it.

Coming from a psych ward, you can guess I had turbulent feelings. I had no structure to my thinking. The chaos of my new view of life was no happy picture. I was decidedly confused and undoubtedly strapped.

A lot had happened in my life to put me in a psych ward in my early twenties. I had fooled around with alcohol and drugs for about ten years. This drug use coupled with the growing awareness of the divisibility of the city and the world as a whole drove me straight up the wall. My expression of life grew to encompass the crazy, and crazy I became.

Just before I went into the hospital, I had become psychotic. It was like a trap where my mind inevitably went because of my quest for the unknown. Finally, I had found out what it's like to be insane. I had always wondered.

My parents had taken me to the psych ward. They were quite scared about what had happened to me. I was in a different world from where I had been. Insanity was the last refuge from the harsh realities of the city. I still had an identity; I was insane.

It was a hard struggle to go back to my apartment and face my friends. I felt like I had failed them somehow by going insane. The only thing that really helped is that I didn't think I was really crazy. Embarrassment was there, but it took a backseat to my need to survive. My roommates didn't want to hear about my stay in the hospital, and I didn't want to tell them. It was very painful and too revealing of inner hurts and pains.

A girl named Ellie, who was a good friend, found out I had been in the hospital, and she expressed concern. I could tell, though, that she was nervous talking about it.

Tara, the girl I had been dating until recently, wouldn't even talk to me. I had called her on the phone when I was in the hospital, and she told me she didn't think I was crazy but that I felt guilty about something.

The experience of being a patient in a psych ward was humbling to me. I had grown up proud and somewhat of a fighter by living in the city all my life. The reality of being judged insane was a shock in many ways, some of which did not settle in this twenty-two-year-old's thinking. I had to admit that the occurrence shook me to the core. I really didn't know which direction to head. It had all happened so fast, and I knew that I was done with the university because I had my diploma. However, city life would challenge me now much more than before. I really didn't know what end was up.

14

AFTER I HAD been at home awhile and had gotten back a bartending job at the hotel where I had worked to put myself through the university, I figured I would go to the library. I wanted a sense of peace in my mind, and I thought by reading I could recapture what in my mind had been lost through my psychotic break. I had a firm determination to go forward in my life and to live out some of the ideals and dreams I had.

I wanted to get a book on a famous person. I thought that maybe I could learn something about which road I should go down in my life. I decided to go to the downtown library, because it was centrally located.

The city bus heaved down the asphalt road with quiet patience despite its weight. I sat alone with the twenty people who stared into space as though it were free. I looked around and saw inquisitive and strangely understanding faces. I didn't notice too much around me, though, because my mind was imbued with ideas instilled by my college education. I had been a student not over a year ago.

I was asking myself if I were really insane. If I were, would I know it? How could I know I was insane if I had the ability to question it? The insanity in my mind was coupled with the confusion of the city. Maybe they were related. I was so crazy that I felt the city was confused because I was personally confused. In some ways, I carried the weight of the city's burdens. What happened to the significance of all that I learned in college?

"We are sure getting a lot of rain." An older man in the seat in front of me had turned around and spoken.

"I'm not complaining," I countered.

"No. Complaining doesn't help," he said.

In a short while, the bus came to my stop.

"Take care," said the man. There must have been something that he thought he saw in me, because he had taken notice of me the whole bus ride. It was as though the bum I had seen as a sixth grader had been resurrected and was now talking to me.

But then I thought everybody knew me. Before I went to the psychiatric ward, I had worked my bartending job downtown, where I had opened my heart and soul to the world in a spiritual way. I didn't think I had any limitations as to my love reaching people. I felt I had the spirit of Christ in me at that time, and I had done everything I could to convey it to the people in the bar as well as the general public of the world and city. I felt that I was sending out love waves to everyone. I was under the firm assumption that my love had reached around the world and touched everyone in the city. It didn't surprise me that the man talked to me.

This belief I had about my love didn't stop the situation from being tenuous, though. In the hospital, I had to let go of the feeling I had acquired in the bar. The doctors were calling me psychotic, and I had resisted. I thought my love was real and had basis in reality, and the doctors had wanted to call it delusional. I had tried to maintain a grip, but the doctors were threatening to lock me up for life, so I let go of my spot and assumed an outward appearance of cooperation even though I secretly still believed in my love for all humanity. I took medication and participated in the groups so I could get out of the hospital back into the city.

When I got off the bus and headed for the library, I felt like I was on stage. The scene was set, and I was the principal actor. This would seem ludicrous to the normal person, but the truth was so heavy in my heart that it didn't seem preposterous to me. It had been a process of reading messages into the music I listened to. All the other people had the look in their eyes like they were expecting this love out of me, but I had let go in the hospital. I did not have the feeling anymore. I was void. However, I must have had a look about me, because the people expected so much from me.

The situation was indeed tenuous. I was out of my mind, really, and right on the edge, but inside, I was a parched, burned, broken vessel. In the library, the signs read History, Sociology, and so on. I cruised through the entrance and went up to the Art & Music section. I wanted to get a book on Bob Dylan, my boyhood idol. There were many people in the library; my head was spinning.

Something had changed in the way I saw people from the time before I went to the hospital to the present. Before, I used to know where I stood with people and what was sane and what wasn't. Now I saw people with a different awareness that I never realized before. I had previously been blind to them.

I saw people having to work at life. I had had a sense of amusement about such people before, because I didn't really understand them as I did now. I didn't stand out for the way I was dressed. I wore blue jeans that were faded but clean. I wore blue bumper tennis shoes that were slight hints of my rebellious nature.

Only nostalgic hippies like me still wore bumper tennis shoes that had been popular way back when I was still in grade school. My shirt was from Door County, Wisconsin. It had been a present from Tom People for taking care of his house when he went on a trip. I didn't dress to make a statement; my clothes were comfortable and not high style. I hadn't dressed in style since my parents stopped buying clothes for me in junior high. Style didn't matter much to me anymore; I was only concerned about dressing neatly. I accepted my appearance and was considered good looking by some of the girls I had known. I wasn't a hunk, but I wasn't a wimp, either.

As I mentioned, the people in the library looked like they expected something from me. I had never been confronted before by people's expectations of me. I had coasted through life maybe meeting small expectations, but I never had hardship or been so vividly demanded of before. Of course, nobody said anything to me; it was something I read in their eyes. Everybody demanded something different but all at the same time.

I was somewhat braced for it, because it had been that way in the bar where I had worked—except then I had had a feeling to convey. Now I only had an idea.

To explain it further, I must explain that I had been on a sheer high before going into the hospital. I had sought the sun, a solution above the sweat and toil of everyday life. I had set out to follow Christ and become like him. I wasn't aware of the ramifications when I began this pursuit, and I still wasn't aware of the ramifications except that I had no cover in my life anymore. I felt like I was transparent.

This was a new sensation to me. I had always been able to mask my feelings before. In fact, I had enjoyed doing it. I had taken pleasure in putting people on and then bursting out in laughter. In junior high and high school, I had been quite a comedian. I remember when my friends and I would resuscitate a dull party with laughter.

Now I was feeling uneasy and not at all funny. Instead, I saw great hope and deep possibilities of joy. It wasn't funny. It was a close, vital feeling. I was empty and lifeless but held a memory of something great. The something great was like a vision of the promised land. I had an idea of what it would be like with God in every heart loving in a full, joyous way. This would not be for one hour or one day but every single day for the rest of life.

As I walked through the library, I remembered the vision that I had had when I had pulled everything together in something like one package of this idea. It was a place in my mind where everyone and everything fell into place. It was peaceful, joyous, and way up high. The vision was like standing on a mountain and seeing things from above. It was kind of messianic but very human too. Some people knew this as home—the religious ideal of going back home. I hadn't found home, but I was creating one on my own to which everyone was invited.

I was pretty scattered at this point, however. My psychiatrist in the hospital had worked hard on my relationship with a girl I had as a friend immediately prior to going in the hospital. I had become bound to her emotionally but also physically. The girl was uncomfortable with this, and the doctor had been concerned about it when he found out. He would not let me lean on her. I needed to lean on her, however, because I had parted with that special feeling I had had, and there was nobody that could take her place in my life. She was my tie with a warm feeling.

My direction had been to sacrifice myself, and when it came to either sacrifice my life or give up that direction, I gave it up. I chose to turn a corner that was new in my life, one that I had never taken. It meant, I thought, I had to let go of God entirely, whom I had been clinging to for a sense of direction. I didn't want to let go of God, but to sacrifice any more of my life would have meant permanent residency in a psych ward or state hospital. I had sacrificed to the point of masochism. I just could not see how that would help people—or, more specifically, how that would be love.

I wanted to stay true to love, because that was the path I had taken. I had been in way over my head, but I took every step one at a time and would not move unless I thought it was a step of love. In essence, I had required of myself an argument for love whereby I moved forward with my life. I had gotten the notion to sacrifice by listening to music and reading the Bible.

Anyway, I grabbed the book on Dylan and left the library. It was still cloudy, but I put on sunglasses anyway. I didn't want people to see how crazy I felt. The sparkle in my eye that I had as a youth was cracking in the middle of my pupils. I was unglued, but I romanticized my decline like a forsaken fading light. Every instinct in my body told me to run. Run from Minneapolis. Run from my friends. Run from life. I wasn't particularly suicidal, but I couldn't face life. I was embarrassed, cold, and angry.

At the hospital, I had seethed with rage. I called my doctor every bad name I could think of. I had just wanted to get out of the hospital, because I wanted to reap the love I had sowed in the bar and all over the world. The hospital had been hell.

Letting go of my spot had nearly destroyed my chances for reaping the love I had sown. I could not grow from an empty garden. The seed I had planted was not completely lost, though. I had latched on to music in the hospital, some of my favorite performers. I wasn't really aware of what I was doing from a doctor's point of view, but as far as I was concerned, I was holding on to what I knew. My doctor was trying to fill me with what he knew, but I was more interested in going my direction.

I felt myself being separated from my friendships with others. These were people I had known a long time. It hurt tremendously to feel relationships severed. I did not have my own base to rely on. I had never developed that.

I tried to remain calm and to stay cool. I thought the whole world was literally in hell and that I had brought it there by letting go of God in the hospital. The people in the streets looked like they had lost something special. I thought I was the guilty one. I had to redeem myself, but it was a pretty hefty task. I thought we didn't deserve a God as gracious as he was and that people were furious at me for not hanging on.

I was mad for being hospitalized in the first place. However, I had gone voluntarily. Now out of the hospital, I looked for some kind of sign from people. The city was a myriad of people seeking answers. I became concerned they wouldn't retain hope.

I had been pretty fortunate to be blessed with a lot of friends who came and visited me in the hospital. They provided love for me to carry me up the new corner I had turned. One friend told me I would just have to think my way out of the situation I was in. He didn't treat me like a mental patient but treated me as a friend. He thought I was in trouble.

I didn't consider myself to be really in trouble, though. I kind of took my situation as a challenge. I remembered Jack Nicholson in the movie *One Flew Over the Cuckoo's Nest* and had tried to emulate his position in the mental ward. I had told the other patients they weren't crazy but that they had just been severely hurt.

All these thoughts and ideas clung to my mind as I boarded the city bus. I sat next to a young girl who looked like she could have been in college.

"Nice day," I said.

"Yeah, it's pretty nice," she replied.

"The weather has been okay, I guess."

"Yeah, not bad."

"I thought we were going to get some rain, maybe."

"Yeah."

"Is tomorrow supposed to be nice?"

"I haven't heard."

"I hope it is." I couldn't bring myself to discuss anything but the weather.

She seemed to me like she knew who I was and saw my importance.

Everyone looked that way to me. I just didn't want to talk about the dilemma I felt I had put people into by accepting all that love and then letting go of the spot when I was in the hospital. I thought I had let go of something big like God, and now everyone worried that God was no longer in their lives. Without God, the world was in a precarious situation. I felt like I was going to have to fight my way out. I was of the point of view that I had surrendered my life, and now there was nothing left. I was confused as to what I should do. My emotions were up and down like a yo-yo. I had forced myself to be stable in the hospital, but I wasn't stable really inside. I was angry. I felt like a dragster revving up his engines but never starting out of the gate. Was this the city I had set out to discover in third grade?

When I went home, I talked to my roommate John.

"Well, I went to the library and got a book on Bob Dylan," I said.

"You've been listening to a lot of Dylan on the record player lately," John said.

"Dylan knows what's happening," I said. "He is tuned in to what is going on."

"Oh, he's just another musician," John said. "He's out to make money."

"He accepts the money," I said. "But there's more to him than that. He challenges people with what he plays."

"In what way?" John asked.

"He wants people to put their love and faith on the line," I said.

"On what line?" John asked.

"For God, or him, or your girlfriend, whoever," I replied. "He is a mystery, and he wants to stay that way. He is free of the system."

That's what I secretly had wanted to be—or maybe it wasn't so secret anymore—free of the system but not the city. The system was what everyone was attached to—that is, the way they spent and earned money and the way they spent their time. The system was what people sold their soul to in order to get a house or car or whatever. The system was established by those full of hot air who cared only about their own social ranking. It was a mindless game played by insecure, paranoid, greedy simpletons. The city was something else that I hadn't been able to figure out yet. I just knew I didn't want the system. I had thought the only way to avoid being in the system was to go crazy. That's what I had done. The doctors didn't call me crazy, though. They had special names like *schizophrenic* or *mentally ill*. They felt craziness wasn't my choice but was something I became because of a chemical imbalance in my brain. I was of the opinion that I had chosen to go crazy—that God wanted me to go crazy so I could learn that there was nothing to be afraid of. The hit on the head had led me to new directions of thought.

I found that going crazy wasn't what I had thought it would be. On the one hand, it wasn't as severe as I had guessed. I still had some faculty in my brain. I could, if I tried, know what was best for me. On the other hand, it was more severe than I had thought. Never had I felt such alienation from other people. I felt like I just didn't fit anymore. For the first time in my life ever, I had given up my direction that had been my makeup since I could remember. I had always gone the direction of sacrifice—now was I to become a hypocrite who couldn't live up to his dreams?

For the first time ever, I took a plunge and discovered both that the devil was not going to get me and that God was too pure for my life at that point.

Now in my apartment, I felt I had nothing. Before, my life was intact. Now it was difficult to tell up from down. I decided to go to the store in the morning to get the latest album by Bob Dylan.

15

ON THE WAY home, I was carrying the album *Slow Train Coming* by Bob Dylan as I was getting off the bus. Still thinking that everyone knew me, I looked at the bus driver. He looked at my album and smiled. I got nervous, because I thought he was looking at me strangely. I wondered, *What does this mean? Does he think Bob Dylan's album is about me?* I looked at him questioningly. No words were exchanged, but he nodded and smiled. I thought, *Oh, my word. I've gotten Bob Dylan to believe in me, and now he's dedicated an album to me. The city people expect to understand that?* It seems that in a city when you are insane, everyone is insane; they are more insane than you are. Downtown and on the bus, people looked like they were out of their minds. There seemed to be a need for them to explain themselves to me with a glance. It was as though they looked right through me or tried to. They wanted to say so much. There was so much to say. The way I saw it, the world was teetering. In Minneapolis, there were so many disenchanted faces. I was melted by any kindness that I saw. Well, now I thought I was the great hope left for the world. Nobody looked at me like the situation was any different. If they did, I didn't want to see it.

I went home. Home was an apartment I shared with two friends I had known since high school, John Followup and Scott Flight, and they were not home.

I went in the bathroom and looked in the mirror. I had spent a lot of time lately looking in the mirror. The mirror told me a lot about myself. I needed feedback of some kind, because I just couldn't get the kind I wanted from people. I had to provide my own love for myself or at least channel love and reflect what I wanted to see in these moments in the mirror.

Then I heard someone coming home, so I quickly left the bathroom and went out to see who it was. It was John. John had gone to college, had a degree, and was now a bartender like I was at a downtown bar. He spoke first.

"What are you doing home? Aren't you working today?"

"No, my boss told me I was so crazy I'd better go home." My humor went as far as a toddler walks. My attempt at humor only made John nervous. I guess he recognized the lack of spontaneity, and the attempt at humor about a subject all too real fell flat. He looked unsure what to say.

"Oh, sure," he blurted finally. "When do you work next?" he asked.

"Oh, I work tomorrow, I guess. I'll have to call the bar to find out for sure."

"Don't you even know when you work?"

"Well, I told you I think it's tomorrow. I'll find out. Don't worry."

"Say, how about watching some TV? It will help you relax."

"Oh, I think I'm going out for a walk around Lake Calhoun. It's a nice day. I'll be back for supper."

I didn't feel I could sit still to watch TV. There was so much going on in my mind. John was hard to talk to, because he was so worried about me. The last thing I wanted was anyone to worry about me.

I needed to get down to an environment of nature. I could really differentiate between urban life and nature. Urban life was closing in all around me now. I needed the solitude of nature. Lake Calhoun was private enough to give me some kind of peace of mind.

I felt my happiness ebbing ever so slowly from my life. I felt crazed and estranged from other people. I felt rejected and confused yet strong and convinced that God would return to my life—that is, return if in fact he ever left. When I had let go in the hospital, or thought I let go, I found that there is really no letting go. All you do is see a different aspect of God. If you're trying to do the right thing, certain people can take over. It seemed like some of the musicians were taking over my heart. Their music focused on journeys of the heart, and now it seemed like they wanted to take my heart over. My thinking was not really clear, and the last thing I wanted was somebody to take over my heart. However, I felt my heart was up for grabs. But I was careful how I lent it out.

16

IN THE CITY, there are many who would use another or take advantage of another when that person was vulnerable. I had dealings with prostitutes on many occasions both before and after my hospitalization. I always felt that both parties were vulnerable. It was never really clear if we were using one another or that we merely had found a way around a lot of complications to sex. I never felt I was really using prostitutes; I felt I really cared about them as individuals, and I didn't think what we were doing was strictly wrong even if it was illegal. There were some people that I worked with who told me about going to prostitutes, and I respected these were people, so I felt it was all right for me to do the same. My body really yearned for sex, and the prostitutes were willing, for a fee, to satisfy my needs. I never did anything kinky, just sex. Afterward, if the girls weren't busy, we talked. Mostly we would talk about our dreams and what we really wished for out of life. A lot of the girls were quite nice and enjoyed talking.

I felt like there was a revolution going on. I remember the story of Christ talking to the adulteress, and he hadn't judged her harshly. I didn't judge our situation harshly, either. I thought it was my business and the prostitute's business and nobody else's. Going out with a prostitute seemed adventurous. I was aware that others would judge me strongly for such behavior, though. It was neither virtuous activity nor was it healthy for both parties. I could imagine the women's libbers or church people on my case.

The real thing, though, was that I had a heartache that only a woman's touch could help. I didn't want to involve some innocent, nice girl, so I turned to hookers, which was illegal but probably didn't hurt anybody. I could have tried to be celibate, but in the crowd I was with, that was not the norm.

In many ways, the prostitutes were like me. Society was square. I got along with the hookers fine because— in a sense—we were nonconformists, and we were also on the fringes of the status quo. It was as though society's rules didn't matter. What mattered was having someone to be there. Prostitutes were there for me. I found them open-minded and sometimes even enlightened. Most prostitutes were sympathetic and loving and open to verbal sharing. We talked about everything in our lives. The sexual part made one honest and hard to be deceptive in conversation. Before I went to the hospital, when I went to see a prostitute, it was a really frivolous time. I loved it when they asked me my name. Every time, I had a different one. I had a different job, a different everything. I loved to put them on. After being in the hospital and losing my spot, going to the prostitutes was a more serious affair. I needed them for comfort. I couldn't talk straight to most girls about what I felt, because I was afraid of rejection. As long as I gave prostitutes money, they wouldn't reject me. Even so, the period of time after the hospital was a lonely time. I didn't see any prostitutes—or many people at all, for that matter.

Every person seemed so precious and so different. I would be in conversation with one person somewhere and somebody else would come along, and I would totally lose my concentration. I could barely handle one person at a time, much less a whole city. In another way, I thrived on city life. I liked to be seen about town. I was especially enamored by a girl's smile at me in a public place. I wanted to stay in touch with women.

I often went out places just to see people and be seen. This lifestyle contrasted with my earlier lifestyle of a serious and busy college student. My roommates hardly knew me anymore; I was away so often.

I was trying everything I knew to get back what I once had. I couldn't tell anybody, or it would defeat me. I had had an ability to read people's hearts and say or do something to ease their pain or help them go forward or find at least some common ground. I had always been able to dodge heartache and see the good in people. Most of all, I had always been able to laugh. I could get away with saying almost anything to anybody, and by laughing, I could get my way out of it. Nobody ever trapped me.

Tara was that girl I knew right before I went to the hospital. We were intimate for about one month, and then one night it happened. She said something to me at a vulnerable moment, and my life as I knew it was over. I couldn't go on, because I had been trapped. I had been called on by her to make a decision. She made some comment about all the perverts in the bar, and I felt that if she knew about how I felt about nylons, she'd think I was a pervert too. I was shattered. *This girl I was beginning to love might think of me as a pervert.* It shut me up. I didn't say a word and swallowed my heart. I never knew women had so much power over me until then. I don't think she did it intentionally, but the effect was to stop me in my tracks. I didn't realize the full effect though at first. I just rolled off to sleep. That is what really drove me to insanity. I didn't want to be stopped in the direction I had been going even if it had been decadence and rebellion. In my boyish vigor, I had always thought that girls were endlessly warm and receptive and ultimately conquerable.

It's hard to fathom what a couple of words could do, but I was out on a limb. I didn't have any way to get down. What she said wasn't important, really; it was the tone and then knowing that the city was going to be difficult.

I couldn't accept that for a long time, though, and I fought to overcome the wall I was now up against. I had never thought of city people as perverts. I drove myself crazy trying to run from it, because I didn't want to think about what it meant. It wiped the smile off my face. No longer could I play happy-go-lucky Mr. Nice Guy. Now I was forced to take a position. I felt pegged, for now I knew one person's pain, and if I stretched my logic, I was guilty of her pain. After all, I may have been one of the perverts in her eyes.

I never discussed this with Tara. Either I thought she knew or she didn't know; if she didn't, I sure wasn't going to tell her. To describe my condition, I would say that my life took a turn for the worse—and probably so did hers. It was a sticky situation, and it felt like neither she nor I wanted or could afford to lose.

That's when God came into my life—or, more specifically, when my grannie who had died came back to visit me as an angel. It happened by Minnehaha Falls. At first, I thought I was the Lord or something. Then I wasn't sure, but I decided to keep it to myself. It was the most miraculous experience—right after the car wreck.

There was really no way to tell anyone what had happened. All my life, I had felt this emptiness in my life that was like a gap between what I acted like and what I felt. Now in a strange way, I had felt like things fell into place or totally out of place. How else can one describe the feeling that one is feeling divine revelations and wants to go out in the world and spread love? It sounds off base or off the wall. This divine revelation was really what led me to the mental hospital. I couldn't control my desires to spread love without considering the plight of those already in mental hospitals. In part, I couldn't fear getting ill myself; it felt like the only way to relieve their situation was to become one of them and then show them how to escape their predicament. I'm not really saying that I planned this all out, but it seemed like that's where God led me. That's most nearly what I could decipher out of my experience.

I had been reading in the Bible, and it said the weak and meek will be blessed, which decidedly was not happening in reality in modern United States society. The weak were being stepped on and called mentally ill by the establishment. The Word of God had been turned upside down by many people's efforts.

When I got to the hospital, I discovered that the Word of God was diffused, and it was neglected by many of the doctors. They may have paid lip service as to having a faith, but it was not evident in what they in reality chose to do and say. The doctors were tied into their medications and preconceived notions about how they were to respond to a certain situation. Maybe I was psychotic by the time I got to the hospital, but I was much more than that. The doctor wanted to limit me to his definitions of life, but I could see much more than he. It was frustrating to be caught up in this little world when outside a much bigger world was waiting to be discovered.

However, before I was to get to go out into the real world, I was going to have to play the doctors' tune. I guess they—or, more specifically, my doctor, Dr. Asbestos—didn't feel I was able to cope in the real world.

At the time, I felt that the real reason he didn't want to let me go is because he was afraid I would expose psychiatry as a false profession and that he and others like him would lose their lucrative jobs. So before I sang their song, I prayed to God that he would guide me, that God's strength was my answer, not the medication the doctor wanted me to swallow. The prayer took several days before I truly felt God wanted me to take the medication. I communicated all of this to the doctor and told him I only took the medication to please him, not because I needed it.

In my mind, I was going through with my plan to love everyone. I felt that I would not move forward unless I could do good. I told myself that if I moved forward where I was that the doctors could conceivably lose their jobs, because mental illness would no longer exist. I thought I could cure it by ridding the world of evil. On the surface, it didn't seem clear that to do something that would cause doctors—or, more specifically, psychiatrists—to lose their jobs was good, but I said to myself, *Well, he is going to take my life away from me if I don't do something. He'll keep me locked up forever! I'm going forward with my life, and if the psychiatrists are no longer needed, maybe they can be just ordinary doctors, or maybe they can write a book about their lives. I don't know what, but to take away their job means that a lot of people they are calling crazy might feel better about themselves.*

I balanced the financial interests of the doctors against the human needs of the mentally ill, and I voted for the underdog. I made the corner at the same time deciding that I would protect myself, the mentally ill, and maybe even the doctors by taking the load of mental illness from their shoulders. It was a deeply spiritual moment to take that corner. I then felt I could reason with the doctors and take their medications.

My doctor was happy I had chosen to take medications. Soon after that, I was on my way out of the hospital. When I played the doctor's game, he said he saw improvement in me. It was at that point I got my freedom back.

That was several months earlier. Now I was down by Lake Calhoun seeking some peacefulness. I didn't really want to focus on anything inside of me; I wanted to have a sense of continuity inside. The time spent at the hospital had really blown my mind. I had always been able to convince my friends and family that I was comfortable with myself. That was true even when I felt estranged and split up like I had felt all my life. I could go way back to third grade when I first began to experience this feeling of alienation. I had decided at a young age that I would never be myself; I would always be a servant. Now I had nothing but a big dream. I was asleep in a state of becoming.

In this period of time, I listened to some of the Christian message. It was hard for me to sit still and listen, though. I was quite nervous. Besides that, I felt the preachers hardly knew what they were talking about.

I felt the real prophets were the musicians. The music gave me armor I needed to survive in the city. Rock music supplied a source to channel my energy. I focused on every single word in some cases. The music kept me from drifting into nothingness. The music supplied a certain strength. It seemed as though the musicians knew what I was going through and that I thought their songs had been written just for me.

That thought maybe was grandiose, but I felt every word go through my life. It all made sense. I had to strain sometimes, but I could and maybe had to make everything clear. I mean, if they were singing about a river and a hill, then it was the Mississippi down by Franklin Bridge.

The music was an extension of the musicians, and the timing of me listening to the record related back to the context of my relationship to the musicians. I had never met any of them, but somehow I thought they all knew me. I felt they had made the song, produced the album, and sold it in the store so I would buy it and listen to it and bring everything together in a nice package, and I worked hard at that. I felt a need to integrate life. I didn't want to miss anything, because I was afraid that if I lacked something, I was vulnerable. It would be a blind spot. Vulnerability in a city is not a pleasant thing.

17

EVEN AS I walked down by Lake Calhoun, I was feeling susceptible to hurt coming from other people. Nobody wanted to intentionally hurt me, but if I let my guard down, there would be those who would be nervous and who would lash out. I didn't understand or like it when I couldn't be vulnerable without being attacked, but mostly I was ashamed of my vulnerability.

I concentrated on recapturing my life, which had drifted out of my control. I needed to feel at peace and to feel secure. I may not have put it exactly in those terms, because what I really thought was bothering me was the rain in my life. That's what the musicians said, anyway. They described sorrow figuratively as rain. I didn't want rain in my life. Despite my uneven childhood, I had always been able to look someone in the eye and see a spark. Now in my condition, people began to look confused.

It was not a welcome response, because I was so confused myself. I was mainly waiting for someone to come into my life and say I was okay. If there was one person I needed to hear from, it was Tara; I needed her to say I was okay. This apparently was not something she was going to say, though.

I was left with feeling I wasn't okay because nobody told me I was, and I was left feeling the people weren't okay because they wouldn't tell me differently. I stood at the edge of an abyss and struggled to climb out of it. Even Jesus was going to tell me I was a sinner, and at the time, that didn't feel so good. I had to find a way to amuse myself. Truth was so blunt and full of despair for me.

My pride had been truly hurt by having to let go in the hospital of what I had been holding on to. It was an image I felt that had been cut into. No longer able to reflect joy, I had started to see rain. Reflecting pain was not appreciated by those whose pain I reflected. People could see this hurt my pride. I didn't want to reflect pain.

Down at the lake, I tried to figure out how I could reflect something that was truthful yet not depressing. Love became the answer. I tried to find a way to convey love, but my love was buried so deep. I wanted to reflect the real me. Tara figured into this idea, because I was still in love with her. The problem of lack of communication between us made me extreme. I saw her as all one way and me as all the other. She couldn't slow down to really look at goodness in her life; at least she didn't want to talk about it. She was content to banter with people and not be too deep. I contrasted by trying to find all the goodness in me and other people that I could. I was very involved in trying to create hope and a deeper feeling of goodness.

I tried to rub all the evil out of my life or ignore it and make myself a perfect human being. Tara was content with her imperfections, almost relishing her insecurities. The two of us were almost at a Mexican standoff. We had stopped dating and nearly stopped talking. I would see her when I went to work, because we worked together, but we were growing away from each other even though a physical attraction existed. I pursued a relationship with her so I could get some kind of closure, but Tara was consistently rejecting any kind of meaningful conversation with me.

I wanted to express something and break through in some way.

Finally, I had broken through to her several days before I went to the hospital. I wanted her to feel how much love there was in my heart, which I could only deliver a certain way. There was a big guy who Tara opened her trust up to one night at work. I put pressure on her to express something of what she felt for me. Although her mouth had said no, her heart still said yes to me. I was confused, and I just wanted to talk things out or get back together with her. She rejected me like I was poison ivy when I asked for her sympathy but was calm around me otherwise. Sometimes she was even pleasant. However, she wouldn't let me on the inside of what she had going with this big fellow.

She didn't seem to care about rejecting Satan in her life, and that showed up. She was under the power of some evil forces. It showed up in her life. Although one might think a city boy would understand these things, I didn't. I didn't equate my decadence of alcoholism and drug addiction with Satan worship.

Tara was frivolous with her life, and I could tell she was hurt. She scorned me whenever I tried to amend the situation with the only method I knew, trying to make her understand how much I cared about her. In my twenties, I was not adept at repairing heartaches, especially when I had a giant one of my own. Both of us had heartaches. She wanted to let things pass, but I was determined to make things better.

We finally met heart to heart at work, and that provided me with the sustenance I still needed to live. I attributed a great deal to our meeting of hearts on middle ground and romanticized what had happened.

What happened was that in meeting in the middle, we shared our heartaches and also saw the great emptiness in our relationship. I was trying to drag her into my life of sacrifice and love for humanity, and she was mainly interested in simple joy. I think I scared her.

Here I was now down by Lake Calhoun still waiting for something to happen. I was waiting for Tara to say she loved me or waiting for God to return to earth.

Awaiting God, I took it upon myself to find a way God could return. In life, there were so many things that a pure being like God could not accept. I wanted everyone to witness the beauty and love of God, because the joy had been so close to my heart. When this joy comes alive, one really wants to share it.

Love grows even in a city by sharing. Tara was closest to my heart at that time, and I would phone her even though we weren't dating. In fact, she was dating others. I needed her, though, and despite her discomfort around me, she would talk to me for a short while, anyway.

Tara really wanted to see me be a success, but at the same time, she didn't want to be much of a part of my life.

I had been working on many things, trying to get everything to come to order. I had set things up as if I were God setting up the kingdom of God on earth. I had to have everyone in my life and all from a certain way of entering into my life, through my heart like what I thought Jesus had done

I hung everything out to capture as much as I could.

Some people didn't seem to appreciate that I was trying to get them into my life. However, I tried to be so gentle. I didn't tell people I was trying to get them in my life. I just went ahead.

Most people were in my life whether I liked it or not, and some people truly seemed happy to have a place in my thinking. Yet I wasn't just letting people freely go through my life. I was setting up a way to rise above the confusion of life. I wanted everybody—man, woman, and child . . . even animals—to have a spot in my life where I would try to hold them and nurture them. It was extremely difficult to bring the beauty of life together into one package—one city. There was so much conflict, so many doubts, and so many diversions that held people already. How could I rearrange things the way I thought God wanted me to? It was hard to think I had everyone's individual interests in mind at every moment as I developed this singular focus.

I had let down the barriers that divided people. For example, I was hardly even thinking of nylons anymore. Every time I did think about it, I could only sense the abyss that separated Tara and me. Instead, I thought about creating the perfect city—a utopia on earth.

My stay at the hospital had been rough on this dream, because I was forced to juggle so much in order to survive and keep my idea alive. One of my struggles had always been to keep my love alive. I had been born again in the Christian sense at the hospital, but I hadn't been able to put it into words or even thoughts too well. I had held on to Tara with all my strength, calling her day and night. I didn't want to deal with the stigma of a mental illness. Tara didn't think I was really mentally ill. I had to relate to the other patients somehow, but I really thought the doctors had the problems, not the patients.

Down at Lake Calhoun, there was an outward appearance of searching by people. People were seeking something I figured I had already found. Looking into their eyes, I saw many things. A lot of the people looked secure but unhappy. They didn't want to smile at me. They seemed disgusted. That was how they seemed on the surface, however. Deeper now, I sensed hope and a strong confidence—almost cockiness.

At the same time, I thought everyone was looking for a savior. Somehow, I was convinced it was me—or at least intimately tied up with me. I didn't understand at the time that people didn't think that. I thought they were angry at me for spreading a lot of love, trying to reap it back, and then going to the hospital and letting go of all that precious love that they had given me.

I was very sensitive about this. I felt like an absolute failure with no one in the world to turn to. I turned to everyone and no one. I was absolutely brokenhearted and alone amid a great city. People were all around, but it was as though I had insulation all around me. I held a tight focus. I had a terrible glare in my eye that I would occasionally cast on some unknown city person. My being was immersed in a rage, but my personality had always been happy-go-lucky. I tried hard to laugh.

My broken heart was over Tara, except I didn't know it. At one time, she brought such life and validity to my soul. It had really been madness, but then that's what I had been: mad. The hard thing is that she had brought hope to my madness and had moved in beyond that. Then she was gone.

I had more to contend with than just that relationship, much more. I never thought I was in danger of losing my soul, but now I was worried. My losses were great, and there did not seem to be anything present in the city that was going to replace right away what I had clung to—my parents and friends. Minneapolis seemed to lack soul. It was trying to be cosmopolitan. Everyone was rushing about seemingly on the run without any depth of feeling or openness.

As before, I tried to spread love, but I had an uphill battle to bring what I wanted to a system that was running wild. There were so many stories. How could I ever capture their attention?

People all seemed dead or angry. I knew I had to hold on to my dreams, or I would really lose my mind. My dream was to create a perfect feeling among people so that there would not be all the negatives in life. I wanted to get back on top where I had been before I had been termed insane. I wanted to show everyone how I had conquered this world just like Christ. The hospital situation had nearly taken me out of the mainstream. My friends looked at me searching for something like an answer, but the answer I had was not simple. It was different for every person and full of contradiction— almost hypocritical. In the same moment, I was both crazy and sane. I was in touch with others. I was losing or had already lost my spot. People just did not see me the same, but that was all right. I was growing.

I didn't really want to grow; it was painful. I was a born-again Christian. Integrating my life into the boundaries of a Christian mind was very difficult. I had always been a little insane, but I didn't want to go back to the hospital. I had to go forward. I was trying to be just a little crazy like before, but no one seemed to understand. My jokes didn't seem funny anymore. Now some people would have me be the brunt of jokes. I wasn't for that, either.

Living in the city, I found it very difficult to be a nice guy. Tara was doubtful that I was a nice guy, and at work, it became very tough to see her. It was as though she wished I wasn't there, or if not that, then it was that I could go back to being my old self.

People I waited on in the bar sensed an uneasiness on my part. The going was hard, but I made progress by thinking that I was climbing the mountain of love. There was a jukebox in the bar that I would listen to in order to get inspiration and a sense of direction. From every standpoint, love was the answer. I related the message in the songs to my own life, and I tried to channel the message God had given me into the rhythm of the music. It was my attempt to break through to other people.

I tried not to worry about what others thought, but I was concerned with that in a way because I was trying to teach them something as well as learn from them. In many cases, we exchanged our pearls of wisdom.

Sometimes it would get to be like anger in the tone of things, and I felt frustrated, because I was trying to protect something peaceful. I was hanging on to the tenderness within. It was barely reachable for others to grasp. At the same time, I was climbing out of a great abyss. The mental hospital had left me cold, angry, and empty.

One good thing about my time at the hospital was my relationship with a girl named Diane. We shared a lot of laughter and a lot of emotions. I needed a woman to replace Tara, and Diane had been there. She wasn't attractive; she was mentally retarded and crippled, but she had a wonderful imagination and a fun-loving heart. We listened to a lot of music together. I was just beginning to learn how to share with women. I had only been able to share with Tara in a desperate way. I learned simple sharing with Diane. It was dreamlike.

I had trouble going back to my friends. I didn't know how to effectively share with them. I felt a lot of tension, and I didn't even realize that I needed to share with them. I didn't feel so compelled. I did feel, however, a need to break through. I felt miles apart from where they were.

I couldn't relate to them unless we were drinking. I could still drink with them and have a reasonably comfortable time at least when I wanted to.

The truth was I was still uneasy. I felt very schizo-phrenic and also like a jilted lover. I always wanted to be somewhere else.

It was my priority to hang in there or be lost. I was in touch with a higher level of being than I was used to. I had grown up always mouthing distaste for something meaningful. Now things were meaningful, and I felt out of control

The situation was so big. I worried about every-one in the world, specifically the city. I truly thought I could bring God home and stop all strife. I sensed that God needed someone who was willing to let him take the driver's seat; John Argent Jr. no longer existed. My soul was run by God.

My mind jumped around. I thought if I could only get over that hurdle that was before me, I would have things in control. I just couldn't get over the hurdle Tara had left me with. She kind of left me cold and let me down heavy. My goal was to show her I could get by without her even though I thought about her every day. I was still in love. The hurdle before me was to get over my heartache and be fun like I had been before. My dif-ficulty was that I didn't think God wanted me to cavort around the city as if I had no problems.

At this time, I liked strangers. I spent time in bars after having worked in a bar all day. The bars hopped with action; there was always someone to talk to. Sometimes it went well, and other times, the conversations nearly eclipsed me. I didn't really know what road I was on. I was creating a new one as I walked down an old one. I was trying to bring people along with me, because I felt I could teach them something or relieve them of their troubles.

Most of the people I approached had troubles of one kind or another. I thought a sincere relationship with God was the answer. I believed I was going to lay down the law. I was convinced I would have an effect on people and encourage them onto a spiritual journey.

My own journey was a challenge. The city is a rough place to start out on a spiritual journey. There were so many steps to be taken before I could proceed. I was learning so fast that it hurt my head. There was a sense of direction in me, but I didn't know how to walk.

People helped me. It always seemed as though there was a decision to be made between two things. I was supposed to pick one, but I always tried to pick both. I didn't want to miss anything. A city boy wants experiences.

I grew aware of the so-called underprivileged. Their wisdom was godlike. The bums carried God in their hearts. If the city had a soul, it was to be found among the poor. They were always watching for goodness either in themselves or others. Tough-minded men and women had visions of how life should be. These homeless people had no money, but they had something more precious to me—their love. Their love was toothy, and they lived for the moment.

There were others too.

Before I had gone to the hospital, I had worked with a Hawaiian guy in the bar. He had a mindset that was very strong, but he was also having difficulties that I recognized. When I tried to get him to open up, he told me he couldn't because he had sold his soul to Satan. I was angry at him because he wouldn't acknowledge God's goodness. I wanted to shake him up.

One night, about one month prior to my hospitalization, I took a drive with him, and I tried to get him to shout out his anger. He was a Vietnam vet, and he had a lot of anger. He also told me that he had gotten in a lot of fights and had "gone crazy." This event was so emotional for me that I put it into terms of an exorcism. I believed I had exorcised his demon. I was scared. I had gone home and read Revelations, the story of Christ's second coming. I believed I had lived through the story Revelations told.

I didn't know how to proceed in life; I let Revelations tell me what was going on.

The next day, I saw the Hawaiian guy at work. He asked me where we had gone the night before. He was angry that I had tried to save his soul. I wanted to tell him about what I thought of the experience, but it seemed corny. I just stared at him, and I felt a pull in my gut as I felt his anger trying to intimidate my spirit. I tried to hang tough even though I was very confused.

At this point, I stood my spiritual ground and tried to be true to God. I actually felt, on a certain level, that I had put Satan behind us . . . the world . . . and eventually the city. Now there was nothing left between that Hawaiian guy and me, and he was demanding answers, but I was unable to speak to him. I was trying to win him over to a feeling of goodness, but he had been hurt so much that he was hostile. I felt a need to contain him, because I sensed that he was spreading evil in the bar where I worked. Even after the night I tried my exorcism (of sorts), he seemed to grow back into his evil ways. At the least, I didn't want him to use me in his game. His sinister ways had pleased Tara, which was a great sadness to me. I reacted by trying to win back Tara from him to me and God. Tara was not paying much attention to me anymore. She was mesmerized by the fun that the Hawaiian had offered her. I was too serious for Tara, but I did notice that her eyes still held a light for me. This look in her eyes said yes to me, but her words said no. I was going crazy. I had that break-through to her heart at this time. It happened at the bar where we both worked as did the Hawaiian guy. I sensed that she needed me. I blocked out the Hawaiian guy from being a part of the union and took a leap into Tara's heart of hearts as she leaped into my heart of hearts. We met in this middle union for a brief instant. For me, it was the union of all unions. It was sharing love. I had set up this union in my mind for weeks, and now it was happening. For the first time ever, I sensed Tara's love for me. The experience quenched all my needs to break through to her. I sensed fulfillment. I sensed fire in her heart.

Tara looked surprised at finding a feeling of love in my heart for her as powerful as it was. We didn't stay in this middle union too long; we didn't seal the bond. The Hawaiian guy looked angry that he had been left out of something. I had made some fast moves, but I felt it was right because the Hawaiian had been stealing her away from me slowly with that Satanic stuff, which went against the best interests of Tara in my thinking.

I hadn't been sure how to proceed next. I still felt way in over my head. The meeting of feelings with Tara had been magical. I wanted to protect that feeling with all my might. It was really divine. I had the whole city before me.

That all had happened shortly before I was hospitalized for mental illness. After my hospitalization and after I had gone back to the bar to work, I tried to get the feeling going with Tara. It was buried so deeply within; I had to do a lot of thinking and soul-searching to know how to do it. Sometimes I thought Tara actually didn't have a clue about the whole situation. She wasn't too nice, and she was not mean; we just didn't see eye to eye. Whereas I wanted to talk about it, she didn't. My entire experience as a city boy was resting on Tara, and she was too overwhelmed or unconcerned to help me at all. I tried to reach out to others. Most of the people in the bar where I worked had advice. I felt transparent but would not acknowledge it. I had learned not to talk of my feelings directly. I was too confused myself. I just tried to get grounded and to shoot for a spot like heaven. I always felt heaven was just a little beyond me, and I would shortly reach it. Then I could let others in to what I was really thinking. The help I was getting from customers came in the form of persuasions toward one direction or another. I knew my direction and could tell if I was getting off it or not. Some of the people helped. Other people only caused me inner commotion and agitation.

It was different to try to work out deep feelings in a downtown bar. People wanted to see that I liked them, but I sometimes had difficulty expressing it as directly as they seemed to need. I wanted to approach people at the deep level of love I was feeling. People who were drinking in a bar were a difficult group to try to sow seeds of love in. I was trying to reach out to people, because I felt any seeds of love I now sowed would be reaped later in life. I sensed that I was on a journey, and now was my time to sow.

What had led me to the mental hospital was that I felt those patients had no one who really cared about them or no one who really understood. I wanted to approach them so I could show them a light. I didn't really plan on becoming mentally ill myself; it just happened. Once it did, there was no disguising it. I knew I was crazy. It showed in my eyes.

Now I had the label with me in life. I didn't like it. I tried to remember my dream. It was all I had left. I had been told in the hospital that I had blown my mind on big ideas. It was hard to know how to proceed with a mind that was "blown." Every thought was the product of a defunct mind. I was trapped if I listened to the hospital staff. I decided to go on with my own beliefs in love, and I figured that on the deepest level, I was not crazy. I had some painful adjustments to make, but I was not terminally insane. Something inside of me was a rock. I got along by thinking about my good intentions. I had only become clinically insane because of various factors. At my deepest level, I was about love.

I felt there was something substantial in me even in the darkest moments of so-called insanity that was enduring and stronger than insanity. There was a light that would not go out. Maybe it was the city . . . at least partly.

My doctor didn't seem to recognize it. I hadn't been able to be so eloquent, and maybe that was the problem. I was actually in a state of surprise about the whole situation. I had let go of so much so fast that I couldn't talk rationally about anything. It was a great finding to me to know that there was no final darkness, just a new turn of life.

18

I WANTED TO get better. I was like an angry dog. My relationships weren't clicking. Things were falling flat. My body had sped up, but my mind was very slow. In response to my parents' wishes, I volunteered to go back to the hospital again about six months after my first stay.

Depression hit.

My dreams to make it in a happy-go-lucky route took a beating. I felt feelings I didn't want to feel. I sensed I was losing grace. I was still on a journey with God, still fighting, but it was hard. I felt myself being humiliated, or possibly I was becoming humble.

My stay in the hospital was a little different this time around. I was concerned with what people thought of me. I didn't want them to think I was really mentally ill, so I always told everyone I was doing fine. I still felt

I was on a spiritual journey, so I was attracted to those who I felt had a spiritual way of doing things.

There was a guy, Don, who was kind of tough, and I respected him. I was attracted to his style but was sympathetic to him too because he seemed defeated. All the patients seemed defeated. Only the staff and doctors seemed like they were winning. That's probably because they were getting the money. I felt that was wrong. If they were really there to help us, they should have done so out of the goodness of their hearts. In order to be effective with me, somebody had to be sincere. I thought people were phonies for the most part. I liked some of the mentally ill patients, because they apparently knew it was a crazy world. I didn't like it, though, when they were so intimidated by the doctors.

I was convinced that love or lack of it was the problem. Mental illness was surface stuff. I was still sure I had enough love to solve everyone's problem if I was just given an opportunity. I tried to keep track of all people and my impressions of their needs. This method that I used was for everyone; doctors and staff were included.

I don't think I was on an ego trip by feeling I had the answer. I could feel the power of God within me, leading me on to think these thoughts. I knew that just a little love goes a long way, but my mind was really up against a wall. It was difficult to give love when I felt so stuck. I tried, though, and I learned that things would only get tougher.

After the stay at the hospital, I went home to live with my parents. I was close to suicidal. I would listen to the radio and hear songs of failed love. I thought the people were singing about me! One particular singer asked, "How could someone so big be so small?" That's how I felt—small. At one time, I had felt so big. Now I was totally humiliated and utterly consumed. I was consumed by people who were reaping my endless love. I was dead tired, but to quit meant to die.

I started jogging with some encouragement from my father. I went about a half mile and was exhausted. My heart was heavy. My mind was a jumbled mess of yesterday and tomorrow. It was painful, and I had no idea of where to go. I could barely tolerate myself. I wanted so badly to escape, but no road like that existed for me. I couldn't concentrate on TV. I was only able to listen to the radio. I slept day and night. Everything occurring around me seemed so dark. I spent my time tracing a faint feeling deep inside of me that was I suppose similar to striving after the Holy Grail, only I felt I would find it. I was trying to put things together. It was a time to make sense out of my life. I had been a city boy all my life. I lived for the city. I was developing an understanding. Why this hell? It was so overbearing. My sense of loss and grief were so deep. First it had been Tara, and then the mental hospital, and then the mental hospital again.

The second time had been really tough. I felt I knew now what suffering was all about. The winter months didn't spark me like they did when I was younger and went to the park to skate. Now the winter looked bleak and was parallel to the bleak outlook I was engulfed by. The snowy yards matched the coldness I felt in my heart. The stark cold wind howled around my parents' house where I lay in the basement clinging to my covers. All I could see was the great distance between myself and city life. I wanted to be in a coma or some serene state. There was so much confusion in my mind. I needed solitude like I needed food. I wasn't well.

The split in my soul that I had felt as a youth was now a division so pervasive that I really didn't know where my center was anymore. I had no focus.

On the radio, and as I guessed, city life was going on as normal in its fast and crazy pace, which was, to my way of thinking, discordant. In the worst way, I needed someone to say everything was okay. I only heard about the problems. The problems lived in my being like my lungs. I had to think of solutions. My being had once skyrocketed to the sun; now I had to remember how to get back home.

Home was a religious base. It was an image to believe in. Home was a place where I would have peace. Home was everything and more. I longed for home, but it was distant from me now. I went upstairs from the basement to talk to my father.

"Dad, I can't sleep."

"Have you slept much today?"

"I'm not sure."

"How are you?"

"Dad, I don't know. I'm shaky. I feel almost . . . like . . . suicide."

"John! You have a whole life ahead of you. Stay in there."

"Dad, it's just that I feel so depressed. I was having the time of my life and then this. I don't know if I can make it."

"John, hang in there. You'll realize something more substantial than you ever had. Do you think you can go back downstairs and get some rest?"

I thought my father was trying to get rid of me. It seemed that the situation was really depressing him too. When I went downstairs, I noticed my father had left the door to the garage open. I thought he was trying to get me to asphyxiate myself. I thought he may not really want me to do it, but this situation is in a make-it-or-break-it condition. I froze in my bed, painfully enduring the moments rather than choosing to lose my life.

A heavy heart feels like drowning in a lake. There's not much to say about it; you just want to get to the surface. I always tried, but I had gotten so far down this last stay in the hospital. The situation was complex and yet simple. I was a mess from the struggles and misunderstandings of the doctors. I had no conception of how to put my life together, because all my dreams as a city boy seemed full of holes. Any thrill I had gotten from drugs and alcohol was gone. The only thing that brought me any excitement was sex. I masturbated. It wasn't like a kid getting initiated into it. I could remember being a little flip about sex with prostitutes. Now I needed sex to feel appealing at all. For the first time in my life, a sense of urgency about sex took over. I began to learn that when I jogged, sex was easier.

Jogging also was a routine I needed to get back some order in my life. Running a half mile a day wasn't much, and it wasn't pleasant, either. However, it meant I was trying. It was effort at something, whereas I had always let city life happen to me. Besides, my father jogged each day, so I thought I'd better do something like that too. I guess I was beginning to compare myself to others. I was trying to follow the right people.

Within a couple of days, I was out around the city applying for jobs. I was trying to put the hospital experiences behind me. I landed a good job with the government in a week. In the interview, I had tried to make a lot of eye contact, and apparently this worked. I never mentioned my hospitalizations.

I read the interviewer as someone who was straight and honest. Even if he didn't smile much, he seemed genuinely interested in what I had to say. His eyes seldom moved, and I felt him looking into me as he initiated conversation with his many questions. He didn't get personal with me outwardly but kept the interview strictly on job-related topics. My concentration was good, and I answered all the questions with ease.

Admittedly, I was still torn in my being as I had been all my life. I had broken it down between an inner voice and the outer world—the city. There was a great division between what I felt inside and what was going on outside. The challenge was to stay on top of what was going on outside without losing track of my feelings inside. There was a good deal of confusion in my mind, but in my heart, I was convinced that there was goodness. I tried to concentrate on that; my drive kept me going.

It helped a lot that the man interviewing me just stuck to talking about the "outside." I felt less threatened. Yet somehow, he seemed to reach my "inside" without even stating it or directly acknowledging that this was going on. It was interesting, and I also got the job.

By getting a job, I felt safe. The safety came in having something structured to do every day. I also had the sense of accomplishment that I felt as a result of being able to earn a living. I felt a little good about myself at least for the time being.

Still, the problem persisted in my mind of what to do about all these thoughts running through my mind about my environment. My brain was as active as an NBA Finals basketball game. I had so many compulsions and obsessions. I hadn't gotten over the idea that I was Christlike, either.

At work, everyone's name seemed to tell me about their personality—Chuck Doobull, Matt Styro, Pat Leather, and so forth. Although the names all told a story, the people acted as if nothing was going on. The office seemed so tranquil.

The people were smiling while their hearts appeared broken and diffused. They seemed to be playing some kind of game that I was unsure about.

The staff amused themselves by mental juggling. Mostly we worked, but this work was always counterbalanced with humor. In some moments while everyone else was working, someone would say something witty, which would be followed by a chorus of chitchat from the others. I would think, *Is this it? Is this what life has come to?* The only thing I could do would be to try to stay on the good side of everyone, especially my boss—the one who had interviewed me. I wanted to run away, but common sense held me there. I tried to learn as much as I could about the people I was working with.

During this period, I fought a lot of battles with my spirit. My mind had gone to hell; I conceded that at this point. My spirit, though, was strong. I had a lot of difficulty sitting still in a desk chair. I wanted to be up doing something—like being on stage performing rock and roll. I was bored in the office, and I couldn't get in the routine. I kept thinking that I should be doing something more important. In the eyes of the city, I was a nobody.

I became talkative with the office staff.

"Hey, John, did you hear about the North Stars last night?" one of the coworkers would ask me about the professional hockey team.

"No."

"I didn't, either. I thought maybe you had."

"They probably lost."

"Yeah."

The conversations weren't always thrilling, but they took my mind off my agony. The agony stemmed from the fact that I was working at a clerical-level job when I had believed I was going to be some kind of star in the

Twin Cities. I had been so sure about it and wanted it so desperately.

The love in my life had been so strong. I thought everyone would be attracted to my message, and I would be able to put forth the charm necessary. The dichotomy between this plan and what I was actually doing was so great that it blew my mind worse than it already was. It hurt deeply. I mean, I was working for the government now when I had earlier despised them and raised a fist against their ways. I was trying to do what my doctor, the new one, Dr. Handvolg, told me was best. He had been happy I got a job. He told me the benefits were good. I was trying to start a revolution, not get good benefits. Nonetheless, I found myself here at the government job silently sweating.

I was thinking about my anger. I was afraid of it. I wanted so badly to get over it or around it. I thought that if I just hung in there long enough I would figure out a way to get around it. I walked a tightrope.

I was climbing still. I was climbing the mountain of love. Everything I had set up to happen to me was laid out before me in my mind. I just had to be careful not to make any false moves. I was tested regularly. I kept my cool. The only rules I was playing by were no rules. My life was the absence of rules. I cast them all off in favor of freedom. I was a city boy going on instinct. I wasn't a slob, but I hadn't sorted out all my values, so I didn't really have a philosophy of life. I tried to do the loving thing. I had a sense of a bright star; I tried to follow it regardless of the cost. Other people seemed to be following the same star. It was the secret within all of us.

19

ALL PEOPLE HAD their own messages that they were supposed to follow. I could tell that a lot of people gave up on their internal messages and became bogged down. Usually, the messages people received were so great that they were insurmountable. For example, almost every city boy feels he is being called into professional sports or politics or law enforcement or something else that is grand. It wasn't surprising to me that most people couldn't follow through on their individual messages. Then the city swallowed them up.

I was determined to follow through on mine. I believed that I could help prepare the earth, the city, for Jesus to return. I believed that this was the main goal of all Christians. I viewed myself as a kind of Old Testament prophet with a vision. It wasn't clear what I was doing as a clerk for the federal government, but I was clear that God wanted me to initiate a spiritual rebirth in the world or city. He had shown me so much. Now I was supposed to show others the way.

I started in small ways. I tried to show people their importance by complimenting them on their attributes. I didn't lie to them; I only told them what I really thought. The compliments were truths from deep within me. I certainly didn't want to lie or change the truth. I could find something good to say about everyone I knew. Sometimes I did it with just a look. Other times, I got heavy winded and went into long detail. Most of the time, I just tried to be friendly and natural. I wasn't trying to win points by complimenting people; I felt a need to express my love. I was under a lot of pressure. Giving love generated well-being. I felt God wanted me to be good-natured and kind. It helped me to feel as though I was coming out of the woods and into the flow of the city even if it was just barely into the city. I was very lonely at this time despite being surrounded by people. Conversation in the office was surface level, and I was so deep into my being and trying to work out my life. I had fun at the office, but I sensed a much stronger need to communicate on deeper levels. My being was really thousands of miles beneath everyday city life. There was a strong urge in me to achieve meaning. Most of the time, such a thing was a joke for people.

The desire for meaning was natural to me; it was very hard to express it, though. I would alternate between the feeling I was going somewhere and the feeling I was totally in the wrong situation with my job.

I had been surprised quite a bit by the atmosphere of a daytime job. At my former job of bartending, there hadn't been much that was serious. The differences in the two sets of workers were great. The workers at the government job were serious, structured city people. Instead of having a lot of laughs as we did at the bar, there was talk of families, responsibility, and power. I was amazed that such a system really existed. Maybe this was what the city was . . .

This type of worker was really in the majority of the workers in the city. They worked day hours and drove midsize cars. They had homes to go to and social activities to fill their time. They generally didn't speak unless spoken to. At first, I had been bored.

A little at a time, I began to understand how they took their respective positions. At first, I had seen them as all the same. That wasn't fair, though; they each had their own story. What they were really good at was putting aside their deep pains and frustrations and enjoying life in a fun-loving way.

They all had their coping mechanisms. There was a lot of sarcasm, and then more sarcasm. I found this difficult, because I was so serious at the time. I was able, however, to joke with them while still maintaining the stoicism that masked my confusion, anger, and even hatred. I used a combination of sarcasm and stoicism to fit into the mood of the office, at least partway.

I still had aspirations about which I was too serious to joke or even talk. I wanted to be this great entity. To be that, I had to have love in my heart. I managed to find love in various situations I was confronted with, and that's what really mattered at the time.

It had not been so long ago that I had had such a struggle with love. I had manufactured love when it didn't come naturally. I had built a feeling of love when my love for Tara was basically unrequited. I had been stern, but people had learned to accept me that way, so I didn't totally fail. That was how it was at the bar.

Now at the office, the staff didn't try to force anything out of me. They didn't know anything about my past, either—the happy-go-lucky high schooler or the tortured messianic figure. Their expectations of me were different. It caused me to wonder.

I yearned to be spontaneous. My mood was somewhat wooden. This orientation was not surprising, because I had taken on such a burden. I had set out to solve the world's problems . . . or at least the city's. I wanted to come up with something that would relieve everyone's distress. I wanted to come up with a chant that would reach to the deepest core of everyone and raise them to nirvana or heaven. I would have to get organized.

The troubles were apparent, but a solution was more difficult. It seemed as though everyone wanted money. I had little or almost none. Thinking about what I could offer instead was one of my recurring thoughts. In a spontaneous way, I tried to satisfy my coworkers using love rather than money. I could clearly see what I wanted to do but had a hard time doing it. There were problems. The staff seemed to enjoy life, but it seemed like there was a lot of dissatisfaction on a deeper level. I wasn't the only one wondering why I was there. The others seemed unsure about what they were doing too. There was a general malaise in the office. A spark—something that was inspirational—was absent. Not too many people were living out their dreams—at least not in a way I could understand. People seemed to carry on despite themselves. It appeared that they had lost their focus and were merely going through the steps. I wanted to touch them all deeply so that they would know that somebody really cared in an open way.

Despite the appearance of the routine quality of their lives, they had something I wanted, which was a niche in life. I was torn apart with only a direction to go and a vague formulation of an idea. I responded to people the way I felt in my gut and hoped that someday I would have the mental cognition that went along with it. The people I worked with seemed like they already had this integration of feelings and thoughts. I didn't; I just acted.

Eventually, I became more able to be up front with the staff. It just took time. When I looked at someone, I saw them as the child within. I always tried to reach that, because I considered it much more important than any title or position in society. A lot of people had lost track of their child within. In order to reach it, I had to live as my child within me. This way was hard, because I felt I had been through so much. It was easy to act out in a certain position, such as a clerk, and much more difficult to retain and nurture my child and the child within others.

I felt I had to avoid confrontations, because they always led to bad feelings. I handled my work relationships in an adult way. When someone asked me to do the duplicating, I did the duplicating. No questions were asked. I was hired to do what they asked, and even if I thought I was God, I was still in the position where I had to do what they asked. I was okay with that. I was suffering about other things at the time. I truly felt a deep compassion for others. I had always felt that since childhood. It hurt me to see some people suffering. I took it as a personal obligation to lighten their load. I was taking on the burden of the world. I thought though others had taken it on, I was still feeling it.

At the same time that I was trying to cheer others up, I was trying to cheer myself up. It seemed as though everyone lived in my head. I had no peace—no distance from anyone. I accepted that that was the way I was, and I tried to deal with it. There was always some person needing this or that, but occasionally I ran into a person who was giving something.

I would remember one girl for the rest of my life. At work one day when I was really strung out and feeling I just didn't have enough love in my heart, a girl, Janet, came up to me, said some kind words, and brought me a cup of coffee. She said, "Take it. It's not much, but I can share what I have with you." Her simple gift lifted me for a long time.

I was bad at sharing. I always thought I was going to contaminate the other person. Worse, I thought I would take all their love, because my heart was so hungry, and then they would be left without any love. I walked on eggshells. My best bet was to try to stick with my job.

It wasn't all that easy. One time, my boss called me into his office to give me an assignment. He wanted me to go out to a place of business and investigate some files. This request was like asking Albert Schweitzer to go deer hunting. I just didn't want to go do it; to keep my job, I had to. I had heard other people in the office say, "I pay taxes; so should everyone." I summoned up this feeling in my mind and directed myself to my car in the parking lot. The rock and roll on the radio seemed incongruous with my job at hand. I didn't feel I was selling out my conscience, though, because I felt the need for the tax system; somebody had to go about collecting them.

I figured I might run into some hostility . . . I was right.

When I got to the business, the secretary said, "Oh, it's you from the IRS." I told her I wanted to see the files on a few of the workers. I was going through the files when a man came into the office and challenged me.

He said, "What do you think you're doing?"

"Checking files."

"I suppose you think I've done something illegal."

"I'm not accusing anybody of anything. I'm just looking."

"Yeah, well, you people from the IRS are a bunch of jerks."

This man apparently felt he could avoid taxes that the other people, including me, had to pay. I was in a position of authority. Usually I didn't like that, but here I was in an argument supporting the side of the government. I felt I was in the right . . . which helped. There was not any chance of trying to please this man. I stuck to what I had come out to do and tried to avoid further argument. It was unfortunate the man had not wanted to pay taxes. It wasn't pleasant to play the heavy hand. This man, however, represented confusion to me. If we could have had a cup of coffee together, maybe we could have worked out our differences, but I believed that it was the best thing to stay within my role of investigator and to not argue. I continued my research, finished it, said thank you, and left.

I had made a choice to follow my boss's orders. It was a choice toward conforming, but I thought I had freely chosen that. The pressures of the city caused me to make that choice. I didn't even notice the weather as I drove back to my office.

When I got there, my boss was anxious to see me. He asked me how it went. I felt like I was in a game of one side against the other. I still had empathy in my heart for every human being in the world, including the tax resister, but I also had to make a choice of what I was going to go along with. I didn't agree with someone who flippantly would not pay taxes. I paid them. Most people did. Why shouldn't he? I supported my boss instead of the tax resister. At the same time, I tried hard not to judge him or have any ill will toward him. There was a disagreement but hopefully no hatred. That was bad for the city and for a city boy.

If there was any hatred in my life, it was self-hatred—over many things. I felt so inadequate to do the job I was trying to do. It was no small job to create something like a path in the world for Christ to return or even to return to my own heart. That's what I thought God and Bob Dylan wanted from me. Nobody else seemed ready; I didn't know if I was, either.

Minneapolis was almost heathen in my eyes, which saw the true complexity of the situation. First of all, it seemed as though no one really wanted Christ to come back. He would only tell them things they didn't want to hear. I felt that if they really knew Christ, they wouldn't feel that way, but I was going to have a hard time convincing many people of this.

I had trouble in my own life. I felt a need to be with people. However, it always seemed like so much was a sin. I was not really too excited about moving forward in that direction. It seemed blasphemous. Apparently, other people felt forgiven, but I could not. It would be a long time before I could feel forgiven. I had done some bad things and was very concerned about my salvation both in an afterlife and in the city at present. It was strange. I knew it was strange. It sounded strange to me too to think that God was asking me to create a path in the world for Christ's return. However, that was what my city life experience had brought me to. It must have been the need of city people and the immense disarray I sensed. How was I even going to begin? I was pretty sure that sacrifice was the way to a whole life. Anytime I chose things to work out for my benefit, I was going in the wrong direction—or if not the wrong direction, at least not the best direction. When I sacrificed, I felt like I was going somewhere. In order to get there, I had to walk a very thin tightrope. My goal was to capture the minds of all people and get them to give up their souls to Christ, who I felt would willingly receive them. It was the best way out of the chaos of the city. There did already seem to be a kind of road for Christ's return that some people were aware of, but the average soul was far from ready. Even ones who believed they were ready did not really seem to know what they would offer Christ when he returned. They seemed to think more about what he would do for them. To me, that was upside down.

I was making snap analyses of people. Most people didn't want to talk about God—not when they were on the spot, anyway. The spot is the point in your life where you have to be honest; you just can't lie. I noticed that this spot is heavily guarded by most people. My spot had gone out to the universe and beyond at the hospital. I felt vulnerable, spiritual, and in dire need.

Obviously, I was lost—or maybe I preferred to think that I was found. John Argent Jr. was a scarecrow. Forces stronger than I had taken over. I was scared, but city boys weren't supposed to show fear. I found out that John Argent Jr. was a shadow behind a great light if I could just let the light shine through. John Argent Jr. was a pass in a hockey game or a hand stapling paper in an office. I was a conglomeration of perceptions. I was an empty vessel. Somehow I wanted a social ranking in the city, but I was also interested in this new life I had so painfully discovered. I couldn't see a lot positive in my life at the time; the confines of my mind were punitive like the Olson boy who threatened my spare change years ago. I had no pleasure, and I felt like I was a sinner of the worst caliber. How could I bear to think I was going to single-handedly usher Christ back to the world? And what of the time when I even thought I was Christ? I must have been in some kind of hell. The thing I did have going was memory. I had memory of how things had at one time gone forward, and there had even been genuine laughter. Now I felt the torment of the city like I had never wished on my worst enemy. It was as though each member of the human race paced through my heart on some kind of journey to my mind. I had wanted everyone in my life, and now I had it. People seemed so clumsy and unsure. I took great pains to make sure everyone made it all the way through my life. If I missed one, then I missed them all, and I blamed it all on that one Hawaiian guy who I tried to exorcise and straighten out several years earlier. Never until then did I think my inner life was accessible to strangers.

I also thought about Tara. There was no reconciliation between us. It seemed like the people in the city knew what was going on with me. Lots of these people seemed to be driven to be successful. In order to keep up with them, I had to stay in touch with a feeling of drive. There were others who seemed very depressed and more reflective. I tried to give these people sympathy so I would not become a jerk in their lives. Nobody seemed to be playing for the middle. My mind had to stretch in both directions in order to maintain my stance of loving everyone. I also had to work on my soul. I wanted so deeply to look at people with a look of love, but a lot of the time, my conscience and propriety prevented me. I struggled to maintain a level of proficiency while being bounced around from person to person. The interesting thing was that they all looked like they understood me.

I had some laughs, I guess. People at work could be funny. Danny Faglaw was a real comedian. He had been paralyzed in the Vietnam War and was bitter, but like he told me, at least he knew he was bitter. One day, he came up to me in the office.

"John, I think it's time you and I had a talk. You've been working here a year now without a raise. I want you to go into the manager's office and tell him you want a raise and a promotion. Just tell him all the guys in the office think you are just tops and you are pulling your trump card. Tell the manager you won't tolerate being kicked around anymore. The hour has come."

By saying, "The hour has come," Danny was hitting a nerve he probably didn't even realize. He was appealing to the way my mind worked. I always thought my ship was due in at any time. In some ways, I always thought I was getting somewhere even in conversations I had like the one with Danny. I was defending my ground in my own way, and no one seemed to challenge me—at least not up to the point it really mattered like that Hawaiian or Tara. I was always able to avoid this point, because what mattered was buried so deep no one could touch it. I don't think that most people tried. They were basically concerned about their own lives, and the fact I defended some ground of my own didn't seem to bother them. I was able to stand my ground.

I met some various groups of people at this time in my life. I was looking for a way to free myself of all the pressure I felt, and I put out a certain wavelength to which some women really responded. It was a certain look, but I didn't like using it much, because it didn't feel like me. I didn't have a good grip on myself when I used it, and I would feel guilty. I still wanted to meet women; I just didn't want to put on any airs.

Living in a city, I was going to meet lots of people. I felt a longing for old friendships, but new people were constantly coming into my life. I had room for them because I had room for everyone. That openness was a part of how I was setting up my life. I set up my life as I went along. I found that new people presented different challenges. People I would have passed by in my youth were now seen as complex and worthwhile people. As an example, the people I worked with who were true city people seemed to be full of political opinions, and were emotionally connected and spiritually searching people. I couldn't imagine the wealth that I was presented with in the form of people. The trouble was that I thought I had the answer for them all, only I was not in a position for them to see it. I was frustrated. Their lives were like a labyrinth I had to work through before I could show them what I really possessed. I had to make it in this world before they would listen to me. My present voice was an echo of a dream, not reality. I was going to have to create reality. The reality I would create would be based on experiences I'd had. I wanted everyone to see God as I did, what a spark he was in my otherwise ho-hum life. Such hope, such understanding, such power—everything belonged to him. Now he was asking me to go forth and spread the Word. The Word was so deep in me that I had trouble getting it out. Everyone was different and required a different approach. I was only one body, however, with a lot of territory to cover.

So many spiritual values were hard to talk about. For one thing, I was not always able to achieve what my spirit wanted me to. If I was going to carry the message, I was obligated to live it. My words would ring hollow if I was a phony. No one would listen. The challenge was difficult but sometimes enjoyable. I didn't really know what I wanted to do. Every moment was painful and full of tedium. The source of enjoyment came in light humor or other diversions. I really had to keep my sights on something serious, though. The city was so agitated it was hard to live out my dream for love and peace. About the only people who would receive my love were the prostitutes who I returned to out of a sense of loneliness as well as a physical desire. I told them a lot about what I was thinking. They listened intently and responded in gentle ways. I didn't really care about the illegalities involved; I didn't think it was a bad crime for two consenting adults to love each other this way. We shared secrets and dreams conversing long periods of time after the sex. There was a sense of freedom and/or rebellion in these midnight encounters. I'm sure the girls thought I was crazy, but I thought they were sweet. We weren't jaded; society was. We were escaping it, or so we thought.

Every day, I would go back to my straight job with the government. I sometimes let it show in my eyes about the prostitutes, but no one ever questioned me. I never verbally told anyone, so I could assume no one knew. I did think, however, that people could read my mind. I thought they were so blown away by what I was thinking that they just didn't feel like asking any questions. I still thought the world was on edge waiting to see if I could bring back God or not. No one would speak directly about this, of course, because it would ruin everything. Some people seemed really involved; others were only halfhearted believers. Lots of people wanted me to give up the ball. I hung firm.

I was convinced I was the last chance for humanity. It was a big claim, I know, but I didn't know anyone who had suffered as much as I had or anyone who had undergone a love experience like I had with Tara: two opposites meeting together in the heart. I was sure that if I could win, the whole world would win. My gift was what I possessed from God. No one had the gift that God had given me.

I had shared it along the way to keep it alive. I was cautious to not lose sight of the gift but always kept it in range to get something back. For several days after sharing, I would be scrambling, but the feeling always came back stronger than before. The stronger feeling made me feel stronger. I kept sharing.

On the weekends, I would see prostitutes or old drinking friends. The prostitutes would listen to my stories of how I felt I was Christ. They would smile, and I would be happy because I was getting my story out. When I was with my old drinking friends, I would try to reminisce about the past. It would get my mind off the heavy weight I felt. Prostitutes or friends, they all helped. I still wasn't feeling good, but I told everyone I was okay. I heard that if you acted as if something were true, then it would become true. I treated my mental health this way and called it good in the hopes it would become good. I didn't have time to be sad about the loss of joy I had. Joy was something I had to work for, not something inherent in my nature.

Minneapolis offered opportunities to grow in joy, however. There were many spiritual people, and I ran into them in various places. We often ended up sharing great truths. There was the time, for example, that I ran into a Native American in a bar downtown. He said he wanted America back. I said it would never happen. Then I said I wanted peace and harmony among all people. He said it would never happen. There we sat each negating the others' dreams. Somehow, it brought us closer together.

I had trouble knowing how to proceed. There were so many variables and so many people. I sensed unhappiness or euphoria but not a condition of true joy among other people. I was sure that if we could just get organized, we could have a world party celebrating everyone's love and peace. Certain things like the crime rate got people down. The crime rate could be overcome. We needed to turn criminals into law-abiding citizens. I felt that criminal types were people who had resorted to crime because they had been treated unjustly. I fought for fairness and justice with the goal that every single person on earth could say they were loved.

I also saw how leaders in the past had misled good people down the wrong road. Men like Hitler had set the world going the wrong direction. For me to try to think about straightening out all these Europeans who had been influenced by Hitler's ways and at the same time work with all the problems in America, in the Twin Cities, and with me was a lot to think about. There was also communism, animal rights, and different religions. There seemed to be a conflict in the making, so I got ready to spread myself thin in order to grease the wheels and to absorb hatred so it wouldn't spread. A trick I played in my mind was to try to change all evil to all good. I went to the extreme. So many people were settling for the mundane. I needed to go all out in one direction. The direction was based on love. I acted to increase love in every situation. I tried to do the loving thing in my life. I knew no other love. My guiding light told me what was love, and I felt a feeling when love grew stronger. I was empty as a person, but love was filling me up.

I had an ideal image of Tara—of everyone, for that matter. People seemed to wish they were perfect. No one liked to have their flaws pointed out. I was this way too. If a person didn't want his flaws pointed out, he had to work to keep afloat. As soon as a person was trying, there would be somebody to stick the knife in. I tried to see everyone in their best light, because I thought the world was in chaos, and any disharmony wrecked chances to really become somebody.

God was light as a feather and would not live in a confused personality. People had to tarry to receive the Holy Spirit. This blessing required faith.

Finding people with faith in the city was difficult. I sensed people wanted faith but were hesitant because so many negative things happened. I hung on to a belief that all would work out. I put a lot of trust in people that everything was okay. I found enough people with faith that I could survive.

I was sure, however, that the world was bad off. No one could deny the problems. At the same time, I was working on a faith that the world was going to get better. The present is where things happened, and it took a lot of my effort to stay focused on the present. People seemed scattered, and some people seemed shattered. So many people presented themselves as persons in despair. No bright lights twinkled in their eyes. They rushed about quickly here and there but with heavy hearts. It seemed that something negative was controlling their lives and not the good nature I longed for.

Just when I thought the situation was too desperate to go on, I would run into a kindness from somebody. A person would show me a good turn with no strings attached. My positive feeling grew with such love. I tried to make a mental note that would be concerning the desire to return the favor some day. Every time my heart was touched in a loving way, I knew what was right, and I immediately became intent on reciprocating the benevolence. Finding this kind of love was a surprise among the many lapses in love. Days would pass when nothing happened. I could see myself slipping into a routine life. The direction was like a trip to the dump. My soul needed variation and excitement. One reason I loved the city is that such change always seemed possible. Common knowledge around the city boys was that anything could happen. The different combinations of people had always allowed my interest in life to grow.

I wasn't always desiring change in all things. My relationship with God was something I wanted to grasp on to and not let go of. I mostly wanted to share my experiences with anyone who was willing to hear it. So much of it was so big, however, that I had trouble knowing how to share it. I shared in small ways, not wanting to disturb any sense of direction or my hold on something that was so fleeting. I was trying to find joy amid a lot of pain. I was suffering, and it didn't seem that any human element was going to come to my rescue. I suffered because others were suffering and because I was seeing so many of my weaknesses. There were those who wanted to take me out of my pain, but I felt I had to pay my dues. I didn't feel I was even with everyone else. Also, I was trying to reap love that I had sown. It was dreams that ultimately carried me through the pain.

I dreamed and had faith that everything was going to be all right. I was struggling now, but I could see an end to it. There was a light beckoning me through the darkness, and many teachers revealed themselves along the way. I listened to a lot of music that challenged me. Music with a message inspired a foundation of hope that one day I would overcome it all. It offered a channel for my life's flow. I was pent up in so many ways and was on top of so much desire. I had to find a way to step up. It seemed like I was taking one step forward and two steps backward. I wasn't bothered by that, because essentially I was trying to do the right thing. I didn't want to be caught doing something I didn't feel was right. The tightrope walk I was making made me nervous but also alive. I was taking risks. If I lost everything, I was in serious trouble. I don't think my heart could stand to lose indefinitely, and I didn't think I would. I sensed at sometime I would get victory. I was off the track in some ways, but in other ways, I was right on target. A lot of ideas were floating through the air, and I was involved in sorting them out. I needed to make a statement by standing up for what I believed. I refused to give in to pessimism or apathy. If I could just hang in there, I would get a voice.

Having a voice would mean I was somebody. It would mean I was respected and had an opinion that people would listen to. This attribute was important to me, because my voice would sound my concern for people everywhere. I knew I felt love. It would be hard, however, to achieve one voice that could express it all. I tried to do what I thought Jesus would. His voice always seemed the clearest to me in my walk through the wilderness. He never fell short of what he claimed to be, and he was consistently firm in his path. So many other men waffled or dodged the truth. Jesus never seemed to fail. The hard part was thinking about how to follow his path. I didn't want to be crucified. Still, there was an attraction to his strength. He was the rock who would not roll. And I tried. I tried to see his weaknesses or fallibility. I had compared myself to him, even claiming some victories I had achieved that he hadn't. It seemed ludicrous to me too, but I had to believe in my own achievements at that time. If one didn't believe in himself, he was doomed to ridicule or worse. It seemed like everyone was fighting for a niche. You had to fight or be lost.

One of the problems I had was that I was waiting for someone to come in and take all my heart. People wouldn't; they just bit around the edges. This drove me nuts. Actually, it caused a lot of pain. I wanted to give all of myself, but no one seemed ready to grasp it. I was quite overwhelmed by the task I was trying to accomplish. I had the idea that everything would work out, though, if I could just keep moving and if I could get people to understand me. Also, if I could get Tara back, that would help. I would get two out of three. Tara wasn't going to come back to me.

I could keep moving, though, and I did. I kept busy at work and took a night class at the university. I even went on some dates on the weekends. Things seemed to be forming for me even in the absence of substance. I talked from a memory of who I'd once been because, at that time, I wasn't even sure I existed. The only thing that kept me going was hope. I was like a man on a raft in the ocean who was waiting for a rescue ship. I wanted to stay true to my dream and what I was thinking, but I had to work through the channels. My boss was one of my major channels. He was stern but open-minded. I could discuss stuff with him. I felt he had experienced hardships and had been a victim of prejudice. He seemed readily open to talk about the big picture. He had a grasp of what he thought life was about, and he shared it with me. I found that sharing my ambitions with him made me feel better. I couldn't tell him everything, but things that were worthwhile were expressed. I told him that I was a radical and that I was having troubles because of it. He warned me that that was an uncomfortable road and a stance on which I could get burned. *Getting burned* was his term for getting hurt. I didn't want to get burned, because I couldn't afford to keep losing. I might react or get depressed. I didn't want to feel someone's hate. That's probably how I got into the situation that I found myself in. I had never wanted to hurt anybody or be hurt myself. I had always seen life as an opportunity to encourage others and seek love. I was a sensitive soul.

The city was both a good and a bad place for me to be. There were a lot of people to interact with, but it was so many that it was hard to think of developing a relationship with the group of city people. It was inevitable that I would know some people better than others; however, I always wanted to be in a position that I could be open to knowing all people in the city, if not the world. I just had to go to the extreme because of the nature of the intensity that I was feeling. I wanted challenges, and I wanted to be ready to meet them. By being intense, I was aware of all the opportunities in life in such a way that I could have been distracted if I did not have the focus of Christ and his return firmly lodged in my mind. When I was presented with a new stimulation, I asked myself how it made more of my relationship with God. Every experience had value if

I could use it to strengthen or develop what I already knew. There were so many ways to do this.

Even predictable things like reactions to negative news could be evidence of how others were feeling. The importance of others was drilled into the deepest portions of my being. I was nowhere without others. My whole focus was on others. Other people presented challenges and opportunities. I learned something from every situation involving others.

A conversation could go either way with someone. It could be a burden and a weight, or it could free the spirit. The art of becoming involved with others showed me the way to make communication be freeing. Even in a complex social structure like a city, people desired meaningful dialogue. Even better conversation than the usual unloading of trials and tribulations existed. It was truly a pleasure when two or more people could share excitement over a topic. People who clicked positively for five minutes were a lot better off than people who dumped anger for one hour.

The hard part of good interrelationships was meeting the right people at the right times. Since I had grown up at a distance from knowing myself very well, I found trouble expressing to others now what was really going on with me. My personality was almost a hindrance to my getting to know people better. I was rough. I didn't trust everyone and could not see eye to eye with a lot of people. Now, however, with my desire to love everyone, I was heading in a direction of sharing and of openness. I was expressing myself and letting others express themselves to me. I was finding a way to talk about truth. I didn't kid around much but went straight to the core. I was trying to really get to a feeling. There was a belief in me that if everyone could express himself fully, happiness in the city, state, and planet would grow ad infinitum. Joy had to come out. It was the most necessary emotion.

It was also the most fleeting of all feelings for me at that time. So many things killed joy—the tragedies, the broken relationships, and strained minds all served to diminish joy. Hardship doused joy like an extinguisher puts out fires. I was without joy at all some of the time. The going was tough. Certain types of people presented themselves, however, giving enough of themselves that I could go on. I was almost always open to humor provided that the humor was true humor and not forced.

I was always waiting for a special moment, whether it was something huge like God returning or something everyday like a smile. I was focused on many things, but I really was mostly focused on the moment. I was on a journey within in a lot of ways, but the outside stimulation that the city provided was also important to me so that I could keep balance in my life. I never encountered a situation that wasn't beneficial to me in some way. Although something like bad news could get me down temporarily, I always came back stronger than before. Something tragic, for example, was an opportunity to share a feeling like grief with others. Sharing from the depths within justified superficial living. I was glad I could still care.

The Twin Cities convey a positive image to those who are interested in their ways. The business climate is good, the women are beautiful, and there are four seasons to its year. I had no reason to want to move even though situations were rough. The city would let me work out of my problems as long as I tried. The city protected its citizens from ending up as hopeless people. There were so many different styles of life that all came under the rubric of city dweller. Everyone fit in. The people took care of the city and vice versa. It was nice.

The city had a conscience or at least a code of acceptable behavior. The city folks did not accept everything, and they demanded proper respect. If people were not genuinely good, they at least had to have the aura of being good. It was a city that dictated propriety. If one was going to have any position at all, one had to be somewhat nice or risk rejection and become an outcast. The cleaner you were, the better your chances of making it. People got to the top by conforming to principles greater than themselves. They gave up natural rights to gain citizen rights. For example, if one wanted the police to help them, they had to act a certain way. A person had to be on the side of the law and needed to let it show outwardly in their demeanor.

It wasn't easy to hide things. Others found you out eventually and pegged you. I was very uncomfortable with this, but the privacy that was sacrificed was repaid with acceptance. If you told all your secrets, lived in the light, and smiled a lot, people accepted you.

I still found myself worrying about Tara. All that Satanic stuff back at the bar had me worried about her. I didn't know if it meant she and that Hawaiian guy were going to hell or what. I had a strong feeling about the situation, and it wasn't good. Somehow, Tara seemed to escape the judgment I felt. She didn't seem to care that she had hidden behind the devil and that she was able to find acceptance from others through conning them. She couldn't fathom me, because I loved her. I felt a strange pull downward as though there was no right or wrong, and Tara could have it any way she liked it.

I wasn't going to give up, though. She was using me as if she were saying, "Here is another guy using me!"

I wasn't getting her to be up front like I needed her to be. She was hiding from me, and I couldn't ferret her out. I could have left her alone, but that seemed to say that I condoned her behavior. I wasn't a saint myself, but I never was a devil worshipper, that's for sure. I was deeply concerned about her.

Sometimes I just had to get away from the crowds. I would go to a place like Minnehaha Falls. In the winter, the falls were frozen. One hundred–foot icicles hung from the top edge to the bottom pond below. Nature was a reality with a deep impression in my mind. I could never escape it, but I liked to escape to it.

Relationships with people became complex and difficult, but my relationship with nature did not fluctuate that much. I was always in an inferior position to the power of nature. It could be calm and inviting, but just as quickly it could destroy without so much as a breath. A man could fall over the edge of the falls and be gone—dead amid the tranquil beauty. I respected nature.

I got my perspective back from nature. I would walk down by Minnehaha Creek and think about how I was a solitary being on an immense planet. I wanted to melt into the trees, but I was too wound up to relax. I couldn't forget the fast-paced city on the other side of the hill. Someone would be waiting to interact with me. Someone would be curious about how I was doing. So many pressures arose even in a quiet place.

Temporary relief was better than no relief. I crawled through the woods pumping myself up to meet the challenges of the faces of the Twin Cities.

Back at home, I swung into my form to deal with my parents. I was changing but trying to hold constant against bad changes. My parents gave me a lot of support and encouragement. They didn't really want to be drawn into the world I was in, but they were concerned enough to hear what I was saying. I told them that I thought the world was heading in the wrong direction. People were getting colder and less humane. They agreed with me; however, they couldn't see how they were pulling me away from what I considered to be a warm position into an unfeeling atmosphere. Their talks seemed to lead me out of my feelings and into space. I struggled against chilly vibrations.

I was really heavy with people I met at that time. I was guarded, yes, but I also felt that really sensitive feelings were buried deeply and had to be uncovered gently and probably systematically. I loved nostalgia and was put back by quick, sarcastic expressions. I had big boundaries on my thinking and could not accept life as a joke. I was magnetically attracted to those who seemed to be suffering. I wanted to commiserate. It was too soon to see eye to eye; I needed to talk around my situation, because my answer was so distant from where I was.

I was an airplane still on the runway of a transcontinental flight. I had a flight pattern that was not to be disrupted without jeopardizing the trip.

Others were in my situation, and I met many of them. There was satisfaction and trials in meeting these people who also had not worked their lives through. Sometimes the experience was testy.

There were many teachers on the way. Rock music had its story, the prostitutes had their story, and my friends had another one. I had my own story, and I chose to live it out as I could. The echo of other voices trailed off, but my own voice grew stronger. I rejected some messages but only after reasoned thinking. It was clear I could make mistakes, especially when I let the wrong influences guide me. I was slow at getting better, but I could feel progress. I used every available instinct, muscle, and idea I had. I focused on really solid things like love, promises, and hope to get me through where I was stuck.

I stayed tied into a feeling about Tara, somehow realizing it might never work out. She didn't express love to me even though I felt her strength uplifting me. She was someone to dream on, because she had always been so free and independent. I thought she'd never fall—or if she did fall, she would grip onto a positive force like the love I felt for her.

My idea of love was developed from my relationship with her. She seemed to be such a winner. She was so cool. Part of her aura was that she was a heartbreaker and not a brokenhearted person. Either purposefully or not, she was trying to break my heart. I couldn't break hers, but she was breaking mine.

Minneapolis, or any city, was not a good place to be brokenhearted. A trip to Minnehaha Falls made me think of many laughs over falling in love. To fall in love meant to be swept away—gone.

Girls in general did this to me. I was blown away by their charms. The love force rolled over me, conquering all that was solid. My feet touched the earth, but my head was in the sky. The universe was quickly shrinking. Stars couldn't compete with the love I felt for women.

At the same time, God was still touching my life and giving me power to go on. His love led me to devotion and humility. The universe expanded. I still planted seeds of love, planning to have a harvest at some point. It could be a harvest I would never reap. The time never seemed ripe for me. Maybe I had just sown seeds for Christ to reap if he returned.

I burned when I saw the love to be reaped. It was very difficult to stand at a distance. I wasn't meant to be fulfilled in this life.

The agony twisted my mind until I thought my head would come off. I couldn't sleep, and I overate. All I could think about was the ultimate moment—that being the time when love circled the earth and people rose triumphantly. I cursed the darkness I felt—looking in a mirror, I saw a stranger. I could sense something much better. I had to continue to pay dues. I showed respect when it was asked for and love where it was summoned. I was concerned where it was all leading, but I thought I had already experienced the worst. Everyday things that threw others didn't bother me, because I saw everything as a challenge. The Lord was on my side; I would never go over the edge where evil forces hung out. I felt pain, and at the same time, I built security by offering it to others who seemed even worse off than I. Pain kept me moving.

Minneapolis was a beast. It would devour me if I didn't watch out. Its appetite was endless, and there was no feel for when someone was at the end of their rope. The beast would vacuum them up without so much as a sign. A person had to be careful. I was cautious. My back was against the wall; I felt every blow that was delivered. Blows came from people who carelessly mouthed expressions that seared my soul. The cuts were deep, and I hurt to my feet. The commotion was too high to go over and too low to go under.

I had to stay put and endure. Even taking a bus ride, I would hear curses to my spirit that rubbed me like sandpaper on a burn. If I were to question those who said it, it would be worse. I shut up and fixed my vision forward. It was a strange irony that I had set up my life to love these people who were now tearing me apart. Where was my love to come from?

I went forward believing that the people who trod on me really didn't know what they were doing. I told myself that in the end they would see that I was trying to do the right thing all along. The harsh judgments I imagined would melt away into a pool of tears of forgiveness and love. I pressed on, refusing to give in to resentment or anger. I would overcome.

If people could have read my mind—and I thought they could—then they knew what trouble I was in. I was an average human trying to be Christlike. I was in the depths of my soul where each move, each idea had tremendous weight. I was vulnerable to everything. I didn't want to make a decision to close any doors, because it would seem suicidal. I was at a formative period of life that called for certain cues that could bring me out of despair.

Cues of love and understanding received from outsiders were what I needed the most. I needed acceptance and to be accepting. I needed tolerance and to be tolerant. I had to match everything that came my way, because I needed to be self-sufficient and to pull my weight toward my goal. To get moving, I had to give and receive.

Equal giving was easy in some situations but very difficult in others. How could I repay my mother for giving me life? The dilemma pushed on my conscience like a hard rock song. It thumped. I couldn't claim to give my mother life. The best I could do was to say that she also had been given the free gift, so why should I feel guilty? Another hard situation was to try to match truly great spirits. I had already given up thinking that I would be crucified like Christ; still I wanted—I felt a *need*—to return love to him that was worthy to be accepted by him. I also wanted to match the genius of Bob Dylan. With my humble talents, I would find it difficult to do anything that would touch him the way he had touched me. There were so many bridges to cross before I would have peace of mind. They all appeared at once. I hardly had time to sort it out.

It didn't help that I didn't really know all the time what I was doing. I was trapped in several ways, and I was trying to get out of the trap. First, Tara had me trapped. She was the only person I knew who could conceivably finger me for not being a nice guy. I had undeniably done some things against my conscience in the relationship, and she was going to hold it against me like a judge. Then the prostitutes had me trapped. Once again, I had done something against my better judgment. I knew many people would not have approved and it was against the law. The situation was too tricky to be over with too fast. Then, and most importantly, God had me trapped. He had manifested himself to me so now I could not play dumb. I had to develop a righteous lifestyle. I was new at that and didn't know the price I would have to pay to achieve that. Others could judge, but only I could finally live with what I chose.

I was glad I had a house to live in with a roof over my head while I was going through this ordeal. My parents were kind to let me stay at home even though I was in my midtwenties. They knew the mental hospital had been a setback, and they wanted to see me improve my situation, so they offered me a place in their home. I paid rent to show my appreciation.

At work, things were okay, but I still felt like I was working at a level far beneath me. At times, I would want to walk off the job. I was at a point where I was humiliated by the routine. My mind wasn't on the job.

I thought about Tara or Bob Dylan or the weekend. I liked to talk to some of the employees; however, the bosses were starting to restrict us from doing that. Work became drudgery. I had another way.

I thought about going back to school. I had an undergrad degree. Maybe I could try law school. It was something I thought I was cut out for, so I felt I should follow through. Law school seemed like an answer to a lot of problems. I had been looking for some means of getting ahead, getting recognized, and getting financial security. Lawyers seemed to possess all of this. When I was a bartender, lawyers always seemed to be among my happiest customers. They seemed well adjusted. Why couldn't I be one of them? I decided I would try to get into law school. I liked the image and thought I would like the process.

I eventually got into the University of Minnesota Law School. I worked with the government up until the week before school started. The group wished me good luck, and I left with a sensation that I was rising in the world—tackling new dummies in a march to become successful. I entered the first day of law school determined to be the top student they ever had.

In my torts class, which is a class on personal injuries, the professor called on me, and I answered with a statement about how justice was the goal in every trial.

The professor said yes, justice was important, but that didn't answer the question. I felt deflated.

After class, a couple of law students told me I had blown the answer. They laughed. I ended up with the last laugh, however. The next day in class, the professor started the class by making a formal apology to me.

He said, "Mr. Argent yesterday said that the courts' job was to administer justice. I told him that didn't answer the question. I was wrong. Justice is always the goal of courts. Mr. Argent was right."

I could hardly wait to see those law students who had laughed at me after class. They told me they were truly amazed that a law professor had apologized to me. It was like Nixon's resignation speech in terms of vilification.

I found law school tough. So much studying was required. Every class took so much preparation. The professors poured on the work to test our limits. I studied twelve hours a day.

Some students were philosophical about the experience. They would sit in the lunchroom and talk with each other about the pros and cons of a law degree. Professors' names were batted about like mosquitoes on skin. These students' experiences seemed to be controlled. I was out of control. The whole thing was overwhelming. The professors demanded my entire mind, and I gave it to them the best I could. There were so many shifts in my thinking required to stay with the professors who were molding us into lawyers. They were filling our minds to capacity. I was flooded by all the information coming my way.

I was still allowing things into my mind a certain way. I was still working on my goal to bring Christ back to the world. I was still romancing with prostitutes. So many things I was still doing while under the pressures of first-year law school. I was being tested.

Never before had I felt such intellectual challenge. The students were aggressive and proud of their intellects. They loved to show off. Nobody seemed to have control; the place was a hotbed of hot tongues. It was very competitive. There was no comfort zone.

I was concerned about how I could follow through on my dream. I wondered about this a long time and then looked for some kind of answer from the law students. Finally, I interpreted the answer. If I were truly going to bring back Christ to earth, I was going to have to be a great man. The answer came to me by way of the looks I was getting. The other students expected great things out of each other, and if I was going to follow through on my dream, I was going to have to be great. Now at least I had a tangible direction, even if it seemed difficult.

I couldn't really understand why everyone could not slow down and become more religious to encourage Christ to return, but no one wanted to skip a beat. The students were all climbing their pinnacles of success. Gut feelings didn't have appeal.

I was confused and hurt and angry, but I was also under less than full control. I went along with the suggestion I interpreted of becoming great in order to carry on my dream.

I thought I would have to write incredible tests to rise above the others. It didn't happen. I got mediocre grades, and I felt I had taken out on a great trek only to encounter big trouble. I wasn't going to be great in law school. I just couldn't concentrate on law when I was so concerned about everyone's salvation and wondering about whether so and so was cool enough to be arrogant and still love Jesus in a personal way—be able to come into heaven with pride.

That's what I was thinking about. How could I line up life so everyone could get a full glimpse of God when he came back? I was trying to lead the students to God by example. I was encouraging them with approving glances and admonishing them at other times. I thought my presence was felt, because I was one of the few who really had connections with those people who these future lawyers would seek to serve.

I knew a fair number of people, because I had been gregarious as a youth, and I also used my connection with Bob Dylan. That was the connection that he believed in me and was devoting albums to Jesus in order to start a secret movement. Every time one of the students questioned my social standing, I flashed the look that Bob Dylan believed in me, and that was enough to satisfy. Somebody as successful as Bob Dylan had a lot of clout at law school even if the people didn't really know that that is what I was using to pull me through. People were having such a hard time; they were refreshed just thinking that somebody had it together.

In a sense, I still really felt Bob Dylan believed in me, even if he didn't know it. I thought we would see eye to eye on a lot of things. I thought I had actually overpowered him in New York from Minneapolis with my love, and to preserve integrity, he had turned Christian. When I had exorcised the demon from the heart of that Hawaiian guy from the bar, I had gained tremendous power in certain circles. Working as a bartender, I was, in a sense, public. I thought my vibes may have really reached Bob Dylan in New York, because I was keyed into him with all my might, and as far out as he was, he may have sensed it. Then I thought that the truth was that we were both having a religious experience at the same time; others could just not see it.

I had felt strange talking about it, because it seemed so far out, but the feeling was so strong. It seemed to me that people were tacitly accepting that Dylan and I were seeing God.

I was experiencing a second coming of Christ in my heart, and so was Dylan, and we were both spreading the Word. It was a nice thought if it hadn't caused so much pain. I felt like I was sponsoring Dylan's career with my heart. I had something righteous that he flourished on. The only way I believed it was that my being underwent radical growth to feed Dylan's and others' spiritual hunger. I had hung tough with the Hawaiian, and now I was paying the price. I was sure that if God didn't want it that way, he would stop it himself, or the city would.

Once it was determined that I would not do well in, or even go beyond, my second year at law school, I began to search for another way to carry out my dream. I hoped I would not need to be a lawyer in order to lead people to love. I needed that possibility to be open.

I had really been in law school in order to achieve something. I now questioned why I had to achieve anything. I questioned the value of achieving a rank. Wasn't that trying to be better than others? How was that love? That seemed like bloodlust, and I was against that. On the other hand, I needed to be moving forward. I couldn't be looked down upon if I was going to really love. That would be a shock to my dignity. However, I couldn't look down on others, either. That was just as wrong. I would have to be equal.

When I had been a law student, I had felt as though I had had an enviable slot in life, and I had wanted to share my good fortune with everyone. When I quit law school, it was difficult to feel that esteem. I no longer had the position.

I looked for something else to define me. I had come to realize society was not waiting upon my every breath as I had thought at the time I described at the library. I began to believe they didn't even know who I was—the true case; yet I wanted to follow my dream out, because it was all I had left. In a city, one can be swept away if he or she doesn't have his or her dreams. I still hung on to a loosely defined belief that I had God within me, and it was my job to spread the Word. The stage was not to be set for me; I was to set the stage for others to follow. Maybe a good follower was better than a good leader. I would try to follow Christ's teachings better.

The scene at my parents' house was getting tenuous. I even got in a fight with Keith, who was now bigger than I was. I was getting into arguments with my parents too. They wanted me to seek help for mental illness; I wanted to lie back downstairs in their house and try to think my way out of the situation. The rough edges of my life erupted, and I had trouble achieving a good, uplifting feeling. Pressure hammered at me relentlessly and caused my spirit to go nearly into depression. I hung on to the hope I did have—that God was with me and the city was too. I thought that if I could meditate long enough, I would get peace of mind.

My parents, however, saw things differently. They couldn't see positive things in my life anymore. Even my brothers Fred and Brett had begun to question my abilities and *my dream.*

Brett said, "Don't enable John, Mom. He'll only get worse."

Fred said, "Is John really causing you grief, Dad?"

Finally, my parents asked me to leave their house, and I complied.

I left and took to the streets. I had a vague feeling that I would rise out of the dream I was in and make it reality on the streets. Maybe Bob Dylan would come and find me. It was a strand of my dream that Dylan understood these things. I had always thought he was supernatural in some ways. I felt like he could have said the right thing to me.

I was scared. For the first time in my life, I didn't know where I would be sleeping that night. I was still seeking something I wasn't sure of but something that pulled me in a direction I couldn't explain really to anyone. For the first time in my life, it felt as if the city was rejecting me, but I could sense acceptance if I could just go my direction.

The streets were insane and a tough place to survive. I remembered once again the drunk I had seen as a sixth grader. Now I was eating free meals with people like him. I was still trying to win the look that he had had. Tara, my city-girl lover, had had it too.

The people downtown walked along Nicollet Mall as though they had places to go that I didn't. I guess they did.

I felt so lonely and without stature. People looked almost right through me as if they were negating my heart. Perhaps my love had reached them somehow and they knew. Perhaps I had reached them through the music on the radio or the news on TV or one of the many other ways I had secretly tried to convey my love. It was no use; I was failing now. I hadn't been able to muster law school. I was a bum. No. I had to hang in there. A man shouted out of a car, "Get a haircut!" Maybe he knew I was really trying. Perhaps he thought I didn't belong out on the streets as a bum. How could I conform, though? I had been a radical since fifth grade with Miss Downfall. To give in now was to lose everything I had worked for. Jesus was a radical, wasn't he?

I saw fights on the street, and one night I even got into a fight. It had been at a bar downtown where I had been drinking. I had met two guys and had drunken beer with them all night, but when they were ready to call it quits, I was just beginning.

"No, you're not leaving yet," I said to the tall skinny man.

"What do you mean I am not leaving? I do what I want," he said.

I grabbed him playfully by the coat as he was getting into the cab, to which he responded with a flurry of fists against my head. I was shocked; in self-defense, I warded off the blows. Then, without even thinking, I threw him down on the ground and kicked him once in the head. The fight was broken up before things got worse and before either of us were hurt. As evidence of our insanity, the three of us went out for breakfast afterward, and both of us who fought apologized to each other. Inside my head, though, I was really asking myself a lot of questions—or, more accurately, trying to answer questions that I imagined people in the city were asking. Was this love anymore? What had happened to my peaceful and gentle nature? It was very difficult for me when I felt as though I was still trying to save the world.

I heard Bob Dylan was hanging out in a Minneapolis record store. I determined it was best if I did not go try to talk to him even though I was in some ways trying to emulate his life. I really knew him only through his music.

The biggest problem in my life was that I was losing my sense of humor. Almost nothing was funny. The fight had been so animallike. It didn't have the good nature of my fights in high school with my animalistic friends. I had a big lump in my throat that was getting hard to swallow, but, on the other hand, I was living carefree. I was still a city boy. I was trying to impress the city with the nonchalant manner in which I accepted my fate. If only I could laugh for real.

People didn't seem to know I was sinking. They talked to me just as though the whole situation was normal. The street people would ask me these kinds of questions.

"I wonder if it will snow today?"

"I wonder when the welfare checks will come out this month?"

"Do you want a beer?"

I just tried to protect my balls, which everyone seemed to stare at. I tried to protect my balls, because they affected the way I thought. I don't think my brains were in my pants, really, but if I couldn't get comfortable with my sexuality, I couldn't think.

I still found it hard to think about Tara. I had been so vague about the hurt that had been caused. It seemed to center around sexuality. I had always had that dark secret in my life. I had that hankering for women's nylons. *I liked them.* I didn't know if it was cool in my eyes, and as a city boy, I didn't think I should bring it up with Tara, if in fact she would have even wanted to talk about it. I would have never brought it up with anybody, but Tara had seemed to sense this all. Did she really? I'll never know. She was a city girl. City girls didn't talk about things that weren't cool. This had been the rift in our fragile but explosive relationship. We had been cool but not cool enough to have no problems. That's okay. We had only intended to have a fling. I hadn't handled the sex part right. I remembered when I was young, I sometimes put my mother's nylons on. It had been the easiest way to deal with my lust. I couldn't find it in myself to explain this to Tara, who had expected me to be cooler than that.

Sex wasn't everything, I kept telling myself, or I would have looked pretty stupid trying to exorcise that demon from the Hawaiian. My life had been bigger than mere sex. I had seen a need to deal with the evil side of life. I had even gone extensively into the minds of others to deal with their evil. I, in fact, had fantasized a path through the minds of every human being throughout the world, the universe, *the city*, a path that the Lord would walk on to the highest pinnacle.

I was beyond suicide now. That issue was resolved. I had the city to live for. The buildings downtown looked so square. They stood erect—no sagging, no swaying, while we humans grew older, less attractive, and more dependent on God.

I would leave downtown and go walk by the Mississippi River and stroll along the shores. I felt I would reach my pinnacle. I called it "arriving." I felt I would arrive if I could just capture the beauty of nature and combine it with the city. I wanted to bring my idealized country into this city life I had. I wanted comfort, but I couldn't bring myself to be comforted among others.

The river was beautiful in the fall. The leaves were changing, the squirrels were building their caches, and I was working out my life in a city. My heart was full of problems. My relationship with Tara hadn't been right. I should have let go—no, I should have never had a fetish. It just wasn't right. I hadn't been able to be there for her always. I hadn't always brought sunshine. If only she would let me try again . . . no. The guy from Hawaii had been playing with my mind. He didn't believe in the power of his own evil, really. He had just been there so I could have something greater in my life—a dream of true goodness triumphing over evil—rather than a broken relationship with a city girl. I had viewed him as the Antichrist. He was the evil one, and everyone else was okay. That was a terribly distorted viewpoint, and I was realizing it. I wanted to arrive. To arrive meant to bring everything into manhood that you dreamed you would be in boyhood. I had wanted to be a star—a hockey player, a lawyer or cop, and a father. I had wanted to touch the edge of reality and then go beyond that. I had watched the city move from my definition of it as a geographic location to a place where people were the city and they ran in all kinds of uncontrollable directions. It was still amazing to me that I had some kind of package that I had formulated in my mind about this place. I had accepted all city people. They were all going to heaven in my mind. It was an idea that began with Tara and the guy from Hawaii. I had imagined that they made it; if somebody stuck on Satan could make it, who couldn't? Everyone was good. I had alternately envisioned the Hawaiian as a blue-collar Christ figure who was trying to save the world for the people of color or as a terrible Antichrist chewing out the hearts of the good people with his every word. He was a man of color, and he had told me he wanted to love others. I think he just hadn't realized the dangers of flirting with evil powers. I saw him as though I saw Christ, because he had so attracted Tara that he seemed to possess some strong power like Christ, who had attracted followers. I truly saw him as the Antichrist, but it also gave me opportunity. It had been hard to separate out my life with Tara from his life. I had even fantasized what it was like to love Satan in order to understand this point that he and Tara shared. I had tried to break them apart. Satan was bad for the city. I was the city. It wasn't anyone else but me. I wasn't going to be stopped by Satan.

I had moved from the geographical understandings to a comprehensive understanding to a real individual understanding of the city. I realized that what I knew was what I sensed and perceived. I could only speak about the city from what I knew myself, however limited or as expansive that might be.

I could identify with many of the forces on the fringes of my life that seemed to affect my life. I was interested in how the city was becoming more diverse. I could see people of color asserting their rights, and I tried very hard to be sympathetic and appreciative over what they were saying. They were calling society racist, and I looked deep into my own life to try to rid myself of anything I did that was racially motivated. I didn't want to judge anyone based on racial criteria. I also identified with the prostitutes. How could I even say *prostitutes* as if they were all the same? I had sought to understand them individually and treat them as such. I identified with the expediency they used with sex. I had looked for ways around rules all my life. I had liked the way we had agreed somehow by our own rules to have these sexual experiences even though they were illegal. We had been radicals. It wasn't as though we didn't care about one another. It was interesting and very warming to me that the last time I ever went to a prostitute was when she told me, "Next time, instead of spending your money this way, buy yourself a pair of new boots." She honestly said that. Her pimp would have been mad.

I was still a city boy. I was looking always to expand my world, seek new levels of influence, get a little tougher, love a little more. It was at this time I began to learn that love can be a self-preserving kind of emotion. One can love oneself so that one chooses that love which sustains his or herself. I began looking for a new kind of city girl—one who could express happy things to me.

I hadn't always felt that way about love. I had once thought of love as sacrifice. To love, I thought, one had to give up something. Now, on the streets, I accepted the idea of love as a nurturer and strengthener. I began to feel comfort from Jesus. If there had been a battle in my life to keep everything at bay, to organize it all, to try to control city life my way, it was coming to an end. I maybe couldn't see it, but I was giving my life over to Christ in ways I never had. The city was God.

It was a bright, sunny day down by the river. Here I was like every day I spent out on the streets, but now it was cold and wintry. The wind blew right through my slight body, weary from lack of good nutrition and sleep. I had been wearing the same clothes for a month now. I was embarrassed a bit to think that I, a boy who thought he could become Christ, needed love. Oh man, how I needed love. Where was I going to get it? I turned heavenward.

I was leaving the city behind. I was turning into an upward chute and climbing a ladder that would always take me higher. The city had been like a web over my mind, and now I was breaking it. That's what I thought. If this city life had been some kind of contest, it was ending. My relationship with the city was going to be changing. No more would I be able to look into the eye of the Twin Cities as an open-eyed boy seeking mystery, good and evil, and independence. I was going beyond that now.

Yet I had always wanted the look of the city in my life. I had seen the look in my third-grade teacher, the sadness; in my fifth-grade teacher, the sharpness; in the bum, the truth. Now I knew the price I had to pay to have the look in my eye. I had to die—not literally but figuratively. I had to let go of everything. To arrive meant to actually have nothing. It meant a death of self.

For the first time in my life, I could now explain how the city felt to me. As I was beginning to let go, I sensed the city. It was like a puff off a cigar or a red cobblestone street. It was layered with drugstores, office buildings, and skyscrapers. It was urine-stained snow or a statue of Hubert Humphrey in front of city hall. It was a man walking a German shepherd. It made me feel heavy like coal and wild like a bucking bronco. I was on the edge now. People's eyes became headlights, buildings became bodies, and the snow was cocaine. The city was moving right through my heart.

My heavy thoughts were getting extremely cumbersome. I wanted to do something—to escape. The city—my life—was out of control. That was a bitter thing to swallow. I had wanted love for everyone. How was I going to achieve that now?

In my last effort as a city boy, I walked downtown to a crowded skyway—a walkway over the streets—during the noon rush and took off all my clothes—naked to the city. It was my last desperate plan that all the good people would follow me by taking off their clothes, and we would all be free and have uninhibited sex. If any of these people were really following me, they would join me. I was playing my card. Nobody else disrobed.

The police arrested me in short order. I had accomplished my final act as a city boy. I was insane. It was a harsh feeling in my throat. In jail, I was so out of control that I got into a fight and got my jaw broken. I even drank some of my bodily fluids in an effort to redeem myself and others. Then I went to court. Things were bad.

On the streets, perhaps I had really acted as though I'd been in my idealized country. I had wandered aimlessly. Maybe I had finally blended the city and the country into one. I had let animal passions take over. The fact is that I had been an animal. I was supposed to be a person, not a total animal. It was required that I adjust my view of the city. This was like taking my face off and letting it be rearranged. I was leaving behind the pure idea of the city and going forward into the world of compromise, adult love, and good stewardship as it looked to me at that point. It was mid-January 1984. I was a twenty-nine-year-old with little left.

Then something happened. My life became bigger than that of just another city boy. The city cast a loving eye on me, or at least some people told me they did. I was committed to a halfway house in South Minneapolis for those suffering mental illness. My life was being viewed by others with compassion. I was getting comfort—comfort I would now accept after my long ordeal of being a city boy. Now I was becoming a man, because I was beginning to make decisions and stick by them. I was thinking of myself now in terms of a man. A city boy followed dreams, but a man had to answer to realities of human existence. I was looking at my limitations. I didn't want my childhood to end completely, but I had been arrested, and I had to look at that. *I put the city on hold.* I took myself right out my whole city-boy situation. I had much to face, but I was determined to face it all. I would have much to overcome, including my history with prostitutes, a diagnosis of mental illness, a broken heart, and a broken dream in addition to my broken jaw. I began to look closer at Christ—the real one who lived two thousand years ago—the one who never left me in my worst nightmares. I would take a good look at his command: "Follow me."

How would I do that in the city? I would have to try. Christ was the only man I ever sensed that I truly and fully respected.

My high school friends Tom People, John Follow-up, and Scott Flight came to visit me. My brothers all came too, as did my parents. They all had witnessed a great deal of the difficulty I had had growing up as a city boy in Minneapolis. They could see how the city was now reacting with compassion.

I had an additional way of looking at things. The city now called on me to be an adult. I was to learn about this disease of mental illness. I was to learn about sobriety. I was to learn about women. Now I was becoming a man. I was going to be held responsible for things I did in the future. No more prostitutes, no more drinking, no more foolish behavior of any kind. I had had my last chance. It would be hard to convince people of just what I experienced—besides this book—a lot of it would be kept to myself and those closest to me.

I got a job with an organization serving the mentally ill. It was a radical organization. To live out *my dream,* I became the lead worker on my work crew in less than a year. I began running marathon races. I was a star in a kind of scaled-down way. I was a serious and hard worker. I was running twenty-six-mile races through the city with city people cheering me on. I was winning victories in the city. I became the editor of my company's newsletter. I became a supervisor.

I found a girl at my church who in a sort of way resembled the beautiful Barbara Handsome. I had never known Barbara that well, really, but in a sense, she had been a great part of what I lived for in the city. She was the city's biggest dream—even more than Tara. She had been beautiful. She had been urbane. She had been what I desired. She was a big part of an answer that was forming.

The woman from church grew on me. She brought laughter back into my life. She liked my red hair. In her gentle-country, firm-city kind of way, she was helping me to recover my heart that I had lent out citywide. Maybe in part, I was still acting like a city boy. I was in love.

I had a job. I was involved in athletics. I had a woman in my life. I had survived, and I had won a battle with the city, because I could now see the city in proper perspective. It was everything I had ever perceived it to be—a geographical location and a large group of individuals, but now I had one additional feeling. The city was a spiritual gift. It was meant to be enjoyed and cared for. My boyish perspective of it as an omnipotent force ruling over me seemed obsolete or even silly now. I guess you had to be a city boy to understand it that way, and I was beyond that now. I could look all around me wherever I happened to be, and I sensed a peace. Yes, I was broken. The city had broken me, but I was resurrected. By trusting from the third grade and on that the city could be understood and that I could come to terms with it, I had become right with the city.

As a human being, I was more important in God's eyes than all the buildings, lakes, and houses of the city.

Furthermore, I was just beginning to see that there was more than one city. Yes, that's right—everyone had their own city that existed for them. My city was just one of many. The city I had known as a boy was a city that had been given to me on a loan basis. For various reasons, I had been required to give a lot of it back. The city for me as a city boy had been a pile of sin, passion, environmental pressure, and a lot of what I'll never know. I remember looking out the windows at school onto the city and being mystified. I remember going to Diamond Lake and sensing the country. Minneapolis was now a blur of city and country. The difference for me in being a man was that I could and should make choices now. I was in my midthirties, I guess, when I stopped considering myself a city boy and considered myself to be one of those adults. I was going to try to eke out a portion of the city—just a slice big enough to handle. The city was becoming part of me, and I was just beginning to share mine with others. I could see they were now sharing theirs with me.

The city was actually for adults—people who acted mature and were responsible—as I had known all along.

I had had to cut the umbilical cord. I was like Dorothy in *The Wizard of Oz*; all I had to do was tap my feet to get home. I was done chasing windmills as if I were some kind of Don Quixote.

I would never be *the city*. I was a grown man realizing my powerless position. I put the city in one hand and my life in another. By giving up my identity as a city boy, I had not only made peace, I was able to look back and smile.

And I would always continue to look for people to explore love. There was always a lot of love in the city. I had either given up my dream or perhaps I was now living it. It didn't matter. The storm was over, finished. The sun shone brightly on me as I walked down the street.

Epilogue

THE LAST FEW years of my grandparents' life, we grew quite close to each other. In fact, I was there the night when my grandfather was on his deathbed.

"Grandpa, I'm really going to miss you when you go."

An Alzheimer's patient, my grandfather had found few people to communicate with his last years. I felt he could communicate with me.

We had talked almost daily for the last five years, 1984–1989. He knew I had been through hard times, and he knew I would have a hard time off and on for the rest of my life. In addition, he knew my love for the city and its people. On one visit, he told me, "You're 100 percent."

What exactly he was referring to, I cannot say, but I took it to mean I was okay with him. Somebody who knew me so well thought I was all right. He thought I had become a man.

I knew my father wished I had become a man at a significantly earlier time, like after my first hospitalization for mental illness. He never said much, though, as his approach was to let me live my life as I chose as long as I was okay with the consequences.

A popular rock star used the phrase "Nylon Curtain" in his work. I took heart that perhaps others had also found nylons as challenging. Maybe I wasn't so weird.

And I became right with myself, no longer a boy adrift in the city.

The city was less about me; I was more about the city.

The city was less serious about me; I was more serious about the city.

It was complex.

I was right with the city.

Acknowledgments

I ACKNOWLEDGE THAT *City Boy* would never have been written without much kindness and compassion from a wide variety of people. Certain ones stick in my mind. My parents and my three brothers were always there for me even though my treatment of them in the novel is light. Their influence was huge, and when I talk about "the city," I am certainly including them. I would also like to thank my friends who sought to understand me the best they could even when the going got tough. I am thankful for Tasks Unlimited, my employer, who provided a safe harbor to dock in after my storm. Another person I am indebted to is Joan Ungar, my art therapist, who helped me with my transition from boy to man. I owe a huge debt to the congregation of my church, Hennepin Avenue United Methodist, who helped me structure my struggles and motivate me into spiritual discipline. One person who I never knew except for a couple of minutes, who saved me from a life of hopeless crime and homelessness, by way of a conversation when I was in jail, who called my mother, who in turn got me into the mental health system, will remain a heroine in my memory forever. I am thankful to the police who kept order in the city when it looked to me like there wasn't any. I am thankful to my lawyer and the judge who funneled me into the mental health system when they could have sent me to jail. I appreciate the return on time spent at the Playwright Center where I learned to write to an audience, and especially to Patrick Coyle for his friendship. I want to thank my publisher, Lily Coyle, and her crew for making this happen. And of course, I am thankful for the city of Minneapolis, which is really the people of Minneapolis, who allowed me these experiences (whether they knew or not).